One-Dish Dinners
for
All Seasons

Over 125 Fabulous Meals for Any Day of the Week

One-Dish Dinners

for

All Seasons

*Over 125 Fabulous Meals for
Any Day of the Week*

Allison Dunlap

Pascoe Publishing, Inc.
Rocklin, California

Cover design by Knockout Books
Page design by Melanie Haage Design

Published in the United States of America by
Pascoe Publishing, Inc.
Rocklin, California
http://www.pascoepublishing.com

ISBN: 1-929862-20-2

04   05   06   07   10   9   8   7   6   5   4   3   2   1

Printed in the United States of America

Table of Contents

Chapter 3   One-Dish Dinners Beginning with Beef

Chapter 4   *One-Dish Dinners Beginning with Pork & Lamb*

Chapter 5   One-Dish Dinners
Beginning with Fish & Shellfish

Chapter 6   *Meatless One-Dish Dinners*

Welcome to *One-Dish Dinners for All Seasons*!

With active days and busy lives, my wife, Maryann, and I especially enjoy a hearty one-dish dinner for our evening meals. With just a few basic ingredients, fresh meat or seafood and fresh vegetables or fruit, we delight in putting together nutritious and exceptionally tasty dishes. And, when time is short, it's particularly nice to know that dinner is piping hot and ready when we're ready to eat!

One-Dish Dinners for All Seasons is a collection of recipes that will inspire some delicious meals for your family. Most of these recipes call for cookware or bakeware that provides easy cooking and clean-up and we believe our Ultrex® products are especially suited to these meals. Whether you need a skillet, casserole dish or stovetop saucepan, you'll find the highest quality in Ultrex, as well as a super-easy clean up!

If you would like to add Ultrex pieces to your collection, please visit us at: www.hsn.com, keyword "Ultrex." Check back with us regularly, as we are always adding new products that add to your convenience and enjoyment in the kitchen.

Sincerely,
Art & Maryann Krull

CHAPTER ONE

Introduction

When you think about a "one-dish" dinner, the first thought that comes to mind is, "this will be easy and enjoyable!" And, for many reasons, this is quite true. A one-dish dinner offers the simplicity of preparation. A one-dish dinner offers the ease of cooking one dish instead of several. A one-dish dinner offers an abbreviated clean-up process, with fewer pots and pans to scrub! All in all, a one-dish dinner is a remarkably convenient way to prepare delicious meals for you and your family.

Inside *One-Dish Dinners for All Seasons* you'll find a wide variety of ingredients that can be easily found in the pantry—condensed soups, dried herbs and spices, pasta, rice, sauces and many other "easy-to-use" items. When planning your meals, you may want to consider stocking your pantry with many of these key ingredients so that you'll always have the basics of a good one-dish dinner at hand. The following foods store well and are handy at a moment's notice:

◇ **Rice:** Brown, white, quick-cooking, Arborio, jasmine and other specialty rices.

◇ **Pasta:** Spaghetti, lasagna, rigatoni, macaroni, large shells and other shapes as desired. Couscous cooks very quickly and is easy to store, as well.

◇ **Beans:** All varieties of beans keep well for extended periods of time and act as a superior basis for one-dish dinners. Consider refried beans, black beans, kidney beans, green beans, white beans and chili beans.

◇ **Soups:** Condensed cream of mushroom, cream of celery and cream of chicken soups provide an excellent foundation for sauces. Keep condensed cheese soup on hand to create appetizers and sauces, as well.

◇ **Sauces:** Many prepared sauces offer excellent flavor and can be a base for a delectable one-dish dinner. Keep large jars of spaghetti sauce on hand, Asian chili, soy and hoisin sauces, barbecue sauces, tomato sauces and pastes and other sauces as desired.

◇ **Canned vegetables and fruits:** Although the freshest ingredients offer the best nutritive values, many canned vegetables and fruits can be attractive additions to one-dish dinners. Include jars or cans of mushrooms, peppers and other condiments. Choose the vegetables and fruits your family prefers and keep at least 2 or 3 cans at the ready.

◇ **Herbs & Spices:** Dried herbs and spices keep for about 6 months so they are well worth the value. Choose herb staples such as tarragon, thyme, marjoram, basil and bay leaves and include herb specialties such as saffron (very expensive, but worth it), fennel seed, celery seed, coriander, dill and aniseed. The bountiful flavors of these herbs will add greatly to your one-dish dinners.

Spices such as cinnamon, nutmeg and cloves are essential to the spice rack. Include also vanilla, almond, maple and orange extracts.

◇ **Basic Pantry Goods:** Along with flour, white sugar and potatoes, you'll want to store baking powder, baking soda, cake flour, oatmeal, brown sugar, molasses, horseradish, honey, salad dressings, condiments such as catsup and mustard, browning sauces and prepared polenta.

CHAPTER TWO

One-Dish Dinners Beginning with Poultry

One-dish dinners that begin with chicken or turkey conjure up tantalizing images of home-cooked goodness. The recipes in this chapter will bring back memories of childhood—*Hearty Chicken & Biscuits, Flaky Crust Turkey Pot Pie, Classic Chicken Cacciatore* and *Mom's Turkey Tetrazzini.* You'll also find some of the most delicious new flavor and food combinations—*Gruyere & Cream Sherry Chicken, Pad Thai Chicken Soup* and *Chicken with Caramelized Onions & Penne Pasta.*

Whether you choose traditional favorites or explore new one-dish dinners, you'll find that chicken and turkey make the perfect foundation for excellent meals. A shortcut to many of these one-dish dinners can be to cook the chicken or turkey ahead and freeze it for use on another evening. The frozen meat will keep up to 1 week. In addition, you can stock your pantry with staples and plan ahead by purchasing the produce and fresh fruits and vegetables that you will need during the week. It all adds up to excellent one-dish dinners beginning with poultry!

Gruyere & Cream Sherry Chicken

1 1/2 c. chicken, cooked and shredded

6 small potatoes, peeled and sliced thinly

1/2 lb. button mushrooms, thinly sliced

2 c. Gruyere cheese, separated

2 c. half and half cream

1/4 c. fresh parsley, chopped

2 green onions, finely minced

2 cloves garlic, minced

3 T. cream sherry

1/2 t. salt

1/2 t. white pepper

1/4 c. butter or margarine

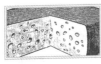 Coat a 9" x 13" baking pan with cooking spray. Layer the chicken, potatoes, mushrooms and 1 cup of the cheese alternately in the pan. Mix together in a small bowl, the cream, parsley, green onions, garlic, sherry, salt and pepper. Blend well. Pour the sauce over the chicken and potato layers and top with the remaining Gruyere cheese. Dot with the butter. Cover the baking pan with aluminum foil and bake at 375°F for 45 minutes. Remove the foil and bake for an additional 15-20 minutes, or until the potatoes are tender and the cheese is lightly browned. Makes 6 servings.

Parisian Chicken Cassoulette

6 c. canned navy beans, undrained

2 chicken breasts, cut into 1-inch pieces

8 oz. cooked lean ham, cubed

3 carrots, peeled and sliced

2 medium onions, chopped

2 stalks celery, sliced

1/4 c. brown sugar, packed

1/2 t. salt

1/2 t. dry mustard

1/4 t. freshly ground black pepper

6 oz. can tomato paste

2 T. dark molasses

1/4 c. water

 In a large baking pan, combine the beans, chicken, ham, carrots, onions and celery. In a small bowl, mix together the brown sugar, salt, mustard, pepper, tomato paste and dark molasses. Add the water and blend completely. Pour the sugar/mustard sauce over the bean mixture and gently toss to combine. Cover the pan with aluminum foil and bake at 350°F for 45-50 minutes, or until the chicken is completely cooked and the cassoulette is heated through. Serves 6-8.

Flaky Crust Turkey Pot Pie

2 c. cooked turkey, cubed

2 c. vegetables of your choice, cooked tender-crisp

(broccoli cuts, carrots, peas, onion, etc.)

10 3/4 oz. can cream of mushroom soup

1/4 c. whipping cream

1 t. salt

1/2 t. black pepper

1 pkg. phyllo pastry

1/2 c. butter or margarine, melted

 Lightly coat a shallow 2 quart baking dish with cooking spray. Combine in a large bowl, the turkey, vegetables, cream of mushroom soup, whipping cream, salt and pepper and blend well. Pour the turkey/vegetable mixture into the baking dish. Remove 1 sheet of phyllo dough from the wrapper and cover the remaining sheets (keep the dough covered to retain the moisture in the sheets of dough). Brush a small amount of melted butter over the sheet and place the dough over the pie. Use your fingers or a small knife to trim the edges of the dough to roughly cover the pan and about 1 inch beyond the diameter of the pan. Repeat with another sheet of phyllo pastry and butter. Trim again to fit the pan, leaving a 1 inch extension. Layer about 10 sheets of phyllo dough over the pie. Cut a small slit in through the phyllo layers. Bake the pie uncovered at 400°F for 30-40 minutes, or until the phyllo is golden and the pie is cooked through.

Kowloon Special Chicken Stir Fry

1 T. sesame oil

2 T. garlic, chopped

1 lb. chicken breast, cut into small strips

1 c. carrots, peeled and sliced

1 green bell pepper, sliced

1/2 c. snow peas, washed and cut in half

2 green onions, thinly sliced

3 T. soy sauce

1 T. cornstarch

1/2 c. water

1/2 t. crushed red pepper

1/2 t. freshly ground black pepper

1 c. fresh bean sprouts, washed and drained

6 c. hot, cooked rice

In a large skillet, sauté the garlic in the oil for 1 minute. Add the chicken strips and carrots and cook for 2 minutes. Add the bell pepper, snow peas and green onions and cook for 2 minutes. In a small bowl, stir together the soy sauce, cornstarch, water, red pepper and black pepper. Mix well and add to the chicken and vegetables. Heat to boiling and stir for 1 minute. Reduce the heat to low and add the bean sprouts. Toss and serve immediately over the rice. Serves 4.

Chicken & Swiss Cheese Quiche

1 10-inch unbaked pastry shell
1 c. Swiss cheese, shredded
2 T. flour
1 T. instant chicken bouillon
1 c. chicken, cooked and cut into
1/2-inch cubes

1 c. milk
4 eggs, beaten
1/4 c. button mushrooms, sliced
1/4 c. white onion, chopped
2 T. green pepper, chopped

Heat the oven to 425°F. Bake the pastry shell for 8 minutes and remove from the oven. Reduce the temperature to 350°F. In a medium bowl, toss the cheese with the flour and chicken bouillon. Add the chicken, milk, eggs, mushrooms, onion and green pepper. Mix well and pour into the prepared pie shell. Bake the quiche for 40-45 minutes. Let stand for 10 minutes. Serves 4.

"Everything in the Refrigerator" Frittata

1/2 lb. turkey sausage, casings removed
2 T. extra virgin olive oil, divided
1/4 c. onion, minced
2 c. zucchini, thinly sliced
1 clove garlic, minced
5 eggs
1/4 c. milk
1 t. salt

1/4 t. black pepper
1/8 t. dried marjoram
3/4 c. black olives, sliced
1 c. cheddar cheese, grated
1 c. cooked rice
8 oz. prepared marinara sauce
Parmesan cheese to taste

Brown the sausage in 1 tablespoon of the olive oil. Remove any excess grease and set aside. Place 1 tablespoon of oil in the same pan and add the onion, zucchini and garlic. Cook and stir over medium heat for 2-3 minutes. Set aside.

In a large bowl, beat the eggs with the milk, salt, pepper and marjoram. Add the olives, cheddar cheese and rice. Add the sautéed vegetables and sausage and mix well. Prepare an ovenproof skillet or large baking pan by lightly coating it with cooking spray. Pour the frittata into the pan and use a spatula to spread the ingredients evenly. Bake at 350°F for 20-30 minutes, or until the frittata is set. Top with the marinara sauce and Parmesan cheese and continue baking for 5-10 minutes. Allow the frittata to stand for 5 minutes before serving. Serves 6.

Chicken with Caramelized Onions & Penne Pasta

2 c. chicken breast, cooked and shredded

1 pkg. penne pasta, cooked al dente and drained

1/2 c. pine nuts, toasted

1 yellow onion, thinly sliced

2 purple onions, thinly sliced

1/4 c. extra virgin olive oil

1/4 c. balsamic vinegar

2 cloves garlic, finely minced

salt and freshly ground black pepper to taste

1 t. fresh basil, minced

1 T. fresh parsley, minced

1 t. fresh oregano, minced

1 t. fresh thyme, minced

1/2 c. goat cheese, crumbled

In a very large mixing bowl, combine the chicken and pasta with the pine nuts. Toss gently. Place the yellow onion and purple onion in a large sauté pan and pour the olive oil over the onions. Cook on high heat, stirring constantly, until the onions are slightly browned and very translucent. Reduce the heat and add the vinegar, garlic, salt and pepper to taste. Remove from the heat and allow the onions to cool slightly.

Place the cooled onions in the bowl with the chicken and pasta. Add the basil, parsley, oregano and thyme, tossing well to combine the flavors. Add the goat cheese and toss lightly again. Serve immediately. Serves 6.

Mom's Turkey Tetrazzini

Crumb Topping:
1/2 c. bread crumbs
2 T. butter, melted
1/4 c. Parmesan cheese, grated

3 T. butter
8 oz. can sliced mushrooms
1 onion, chopped
4 cloves garlic, minced
1/4 t. ground nutmeg
1 T. fresh thyme, minced
1/4 c. flour

2 c. chicken broth
1 c. Parmesan cheese, grated
3 T. dry sherry
2 t. fresh lemon juice
1 t. salt
1/2 t. black pepper
4 c. cooked turkey, cubed
12 oz. linguine, cooked al dente, drained
4 c. broccoli florets, cooked tender-crisp
1/2 c. almonds, sliced and toasted

Prepare the topping by combining the bread crumbs, butter and Parmesan cheese. Set aside. Place the butter in a large sauté pan and melt. Add the mushrooms, onion, garlic, thyme, nutmeg and sauté for 2 minutes. Stir the flour into the mushrooms and gradually add the chicken broth, stirring with a whisk. Bring to a boil and cook for 5 minutes or until thick. Add the cheese, sherry, lemon juice, salt and pepper and stir again. Remove from the heat. Add the turkey and mix well.

Lightly coat a 9" x 13" baking pan with cooking spray. Place one-half of the linguine in the pan. Cover with half of the broccoli and half of the turkey mixture. Repeat the layers. Sprinkle with the bread crumb topping and bake at 450°F for 15 minutes, or until golden brown. Garnish with the toasted almonds to serve. Serves 8.

Alaskan White Chili

1 lb. Great Northern beans, rinsed
6-8 c. chicken broth
2 cloves garlic, minced
2 onions, chopped, divided
1 T. olive oil
1 t. ground cumin
1 t. ground oregano
1/2 t. ground red pepper
2 c. uncooked chicken breast, cubed
8 oz. can green chilies, chopped
sour cream
Jack cheese, shredded
Prepared salsa

 Combine the beans, 6 cups of chicken broth, garlic and 1 onion in a skillet or ovenproof stockpot. Cover and bring to a boil, then simmer for 1 hour. Heat the olive oil in a large skillet and add 1 onion. Add the cumin, oregano and red pepper. Add this onion/spice mixture to the beans. Cover and cook 1-1½ hours or until the beans are very tender. Add additional chicken broth, if needed and stir occasionally. Add the chicken and the green chilies and cook for an additional 15 minutes. To serve, arrange sour cream, Jack cheese and salsa at the table and pass with bowls of the chili. Serves 4.

Autumn Evening Skillet Dinner

1/4 c. extra virgin olive oil	2 T. butter
4 c. frozen diced potatoes	1 c. milk
1 c. onion, chopped	2 t. instant chicken bouillon
1 green pepper, chopped	1 t. freshly ground black pepper
2 c. cooked chicken meat, shredded	1/2 c. cheddar cheese, shredded
2 T. flour	

 Heat the oil until hot in a large skillet. Add the frozen diced potatoes, onion and green pepper and cook until the potatoes are browned. Scatter the chicken over the potatoes and keep warm on low heat. In a small saucepan, combine the flour and butter over medium heat. Stir constantly until the mixture is thickened. Slowly add the milk and bring to a boil. Stir occasionally. Reduce the heat and add the chicken bouillon, pepper and cheddar cheese. Blend well. Pour the sauce over the chicken mixture. Simmer for 2 minutes and serve immediately. Serves 4.

Pad Thai Chicken Soup

3 1/2 qts. chicken broth

1 carrot, peeled and cut into small chunks

1 large yellow onion, quartered

4 whole cloves

1/2 t. whole peppercorns

2 ribs celery, cut into chunks

2-inch piece fresh ginger, peeled and cut in half

3 1/2 lbs. chicken, cleaned and skin removed

1 head Napa cabbage, rinsed, cut into 1-inch strips (10 cups)

3 carrots, peeled and thinly sliced

2 ribs celery, thinly sliced

1/4 lb. pad thai (rice) noodles

8 oz. can water chestnuts, sliced

1/4 c. soy sauce

2 T. hoisin sauce

1 c. bean sprouts, washed and cut in 2-inch pieces

1/2 c. fresh cilantro, chopped

1/2 c. green onions, chopped

In a large stockpot, combine the chicken broth, carrot, onion, cloves, peppercorns, celery, ginger and chicken. Bring to a boil. Partially cover, reduce the heat and simmer for 2 hours. Strain the liquid through a sieve into another large pot. Reserve the broth. Set the chicken aside and discard the other solids. When the chicken is cool enough to handle, remove the meat and discard the bones. Shred the meat into bite-sized pieces.

To assemble the soup, bring the broth to a simmer. Add the cabbage, carrots and celery and simmer for 5 minutes. Add the noodles, simmer for 4 minutes, and add the reserved chicken, water chestnuts, soy sauce, hoisin, bean sprouts and cilantro leaves. Simmer for 3 minutes. Garnish with the green onions and serve immediately. Serves 8.

Stuffed & Double-Stuffed Chicken

6 c. seasoned, cubed herb stuffing

1/2 c. butter or margarine, melted

3 c. boiling water

2 T. fresh parsley, minced

1 medium onion, finely chopped

2 ribs celery, finely chopped

1/4 c. almonds, diced

6 chicken breast halves, boneless and skinless

1 t. paprika

2 c. chicken broth

Parmesan cheese for garnish

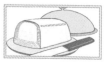

Prepare the stuffing by combining the stuffing, butter and boiling water. Toss well. Add the parsley, onion, celery and almonds. Cut a deep slit sideways in each chicken breast to form a pocket and fill each breast with stuffing. Lightly coat a 9" x 13" pan with cooking spray. Place the chicken breasts in the pan. Sprinkle the paprika over the chicken. Scatter the remaining stuffing mix around the chicken pieces and pour the chicken broth over the stuffing. Sprinkle the Parmesan cheese over all. Cover and bake at 375°F for 45 minutes, or until the chicken is cooked completely through. Serves 6.

Grecian Chicken & Vegetables

1 c. wild rice mix, uncooked	1 t. dried oregano
2 zucchini, sliced	1 t. salt
1 lb. red new potatoes, cleaned and cut into quarters	1/2 t. freshly ground black pepper
2 cloves garlic, minced	4 chicken breast halves, boneless and skinless
2 c. plum tomatoes, diced	3 1/2 c. chicken broth
1 t. dried basil	4 oz. goat cheese, crumbled

 Coat a large baking pan with cooking spray. Spread the rice mix on the bottom of the pan. Arrange the zucchini, new potatoes, garlic and tomatoes in layers over the rice. Sprinkle the basil, oregano, salt and pepper over the vegetables. Place the chicken breasts over the spices. Pour the chicken broth over everything and bake, covered, at 375°F for 45 minutes. Remove the cover and sprinkle the cheese over the top of the chicken and bake for an additional 5-10 minutes, or until the cheese is slightly melted and the chicken is completely cooked. Serves 4.

Turkey & Summer Vegetable Medley

1 T. extra virgin olive oil

1 medium onion, chopped

2 cloves garlic, minced

1 T. flour

1/2 t. salt

1/2 t. black pepper

1/4 t. cayenne pepper

1/2 c. chili sauce

16 oz. can diced tomatoes, undrained

1 lb. turkey tenderloin, cut into 4 pieces

4 ears corn-on-the-cob, fresh or frozen and thawed

1 green bell pepper, sliced

Parmesan cheese to taste

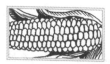 In a large skillet, heat the oil and add the onion and garlic. Sauté for 2 minutes. Add the flour, salt, pepper, cayenne pepper, chili sauce and diced tomatoes and mix well. Place the turkey pieces in the sauce and add the corn, arranging the foods evenly in the pan. Bring to a boil and reduce the heat to low. Cover and simmer 20 minutes, or until the turkey is completely cooked. Add the green pepper and simmer for 3 minutes. Sprinkle the Parmesan cheese over all and serve immediately. Serves 4.

Hearty Chicken & Biscuits

6 c. cooked chicken, cut into small pieces	2 14-1/2 oz. cans chicken broth
1 c. onion, chopped	1/3 c. cornstarch
1 c. celery, chopped	3/4 c. water
1 c. red pepper, chopped	4 c. prepared baking mix
1 c. broccoli florets, chopped	1 1/2 c. milk
1 c. carrots, peeled and cubed	2 T. sugar
	1 T. fresh parsley, minced

 Using a large saucepan, heat the chicken, onion, celery, red pepper, broccoli, carrots and chicken broth to boiling. In a small bowl, mix the cornstarch with the water until well-blended and slowly add to the boiling broth. Stir until the mixture boils again and the broth is thickened. Boil 1 minute. Remove from the heat and pour the chicken and vegetables into a 9" x 13" baking pan.

Combine the baking mix, milk, sugar and parsley in a medium bowl and mix until no lumps remain. Using a soup spoon, drop biscuits the size of large walnuts over the chicken and vegetables, covering the top of the baking pan completely. Bake, uncovered, at 400°F for 25-30 minutes, or until the biscuits are cooked through. Serves 6.

Sour Cream Chicken & Noodles

2 T. extra virgin olive oil

1 c. onion, chopped

2 c. dairy sour cream

1/2 c. milk

1 t. salt

1/2 t. freshly ground black pepper

2 c. cooked chicken breast, cut into small cubes

4 oz. can mushrooms, sliced, drained

1 c. frozen peas

8 oz. wide egg noodles, cooked and drained

1/2 c. Parmesan cheese, grated

 In a medium sauté pan, heat the oil and add the onion. Sauté for 2 minutes, or until the onions are translucent. Add the sour cream, milk, salt, pepper, chicken, mushrooms and peas and cook for 2 minutes. Add the noodles and mix again. Lightly coat a 2-quart baking pan with cooking spray and pour the chicken and noodles into the pan. Sprinkle the Parmesan cheese over all and bake at 350°F for 30-35 minutes. Serves 6.

Countryside Chicken Dinner

4 bone-in chicken breasts, skinless

2 carrots, peeled, cut in 1-inch pieces

4 shallots, peeled and cut in half

6 baby new potatoes, scrubbed and cut in half

1 c. fresh green beans, cut in 1-inch pieces

2 cloves garlic, minced

14.5 oz. can chicken broth

1 t. dried Italian seasoning

1 t. salt

1 t. black pepper

Place the chicken breasts in a large baking pan. Arrange the carrots, shallots, potatoes and green beans around the chicken pieces. Sprinkle the garlic over the chicken and vegetables and pour the chicken broth over all. Sprinkle the Italian seasoning, salt and pepper over the broth. Cover and bake at 350°F for 60 minutes, or until the chicken is completely cooked through. Serves 4.

Asparagus & Wild Rice Chicken

1 c. wild rice mix

4 chicken breast halves

1 large Vidalia onion, cut into 6 wedges

1 lb. asparagus, trimmed and cut into 2-inch pieces

3 c. chicken broth

2 T. extra virgin olive oil

1 T. rice wine vinegar

1 T. garlic, minced

1/2 t. salt

1/4 t. black pepper

Coat a large baking pan with cooking spray. Place the rice in the bottom of the pan. Add the chicken over the rice. Arrange the onion and asparagus around the chicken and pour the chicken broth over all. Mix together in a small bowl, the olive oil, rice wine vinegar, garlic, salt and pepper. Add to the chicken mixture. Cover tightly and bake at 375°F for 1 hour, or until the chicken is cooked completely through. Serves 4.

Coq Au Vin

8 slices bacon

1 c. flour

1 t. dried Italian seasoning

1 t. freshly ground black pepper

8 slices bacon

3-4 lb. fryer chicken, cut into pieces

4 large onions, peeled and cut into fourths

4 large carrots, peeled and cut into 2-inch pieces

2 large potatoes, peeled and cut into 1-inch pieces

2 c. Chianti (or dry red wine of your choice)

 Fry the bacon in a large skillet until fully cooked. Remove from the pan and crumble. Set aside. Combine the flour, Italian seasoning and black pepper in a large plastic bag and dredge each piece of chicken in the flour and seasonings. Heat the bacon drippings to medium-high heat and place the chicken in the skillet. Cook over medium-high heat for 6-7 minutes, turning once to brown evenly. Remove the chicken from the skillet. Place the onions, carrots and potatoes in the skillet and cook over medium heat for 5 minutes. Add the Chianti, chicken and bacon pieces and simmer for 35 minutes, covered, until the chicken is completely cooked and the vegetables are tender. Serves 4-6.

Classic Chicken Cacciatore

1 c. flour

1 t. salt

1/2 t. black pepper

1/2 t. ground paprika

3-4 lb. roasting chicken, cut into pieces

3 T. vegetable oil

1 medium onion, chopped

3 cloves garlic, minced

1/2 lb. mushrooms, sliced

14 1/2 oz. can diced tomatoes, undrained

6 oz. can tomato paste

1/4 c. Marsala wine

1 t. dried basil

1/2 t. ground oregano

1/2 t. ground marjoram

1/4 t. dried rosemary

1 c. canned green beans (or frozen, thawed green beans)

1 lb. spaghettini noodles, cooked al dente

Parmesan cheese

In a large plastic bag, combine the flour, salt, pepper and paprika. Dredge each piece of chicken in the flour mixture. Heat the oil in a large stockpot until hot. Add the chicken pieces and cook over medium-high heat for 6-7 minutes, turning the chicken as it browns. Remove the chicken and set aside. Sauté the onions and garlic in the pan drippings for 2-3 minutes, or until translucent. Add the mushrooms, tomatoes, tomato paste and stir to mix well. Add the wine, basil, oregano, marjoram and rosemary and mix again. Add the chicken pieces, cover and simmer for 30-35 minutes, or until the chicken is completely cooked through. Add the green beans and cook for an additional 5 minutes. To serve, place equal portions of spaghettini noodles on 4 plates. Top with the chicken and cacciatore sauce and garnish with the Parmesan cheese. Makes 4 servings.

Mediterranean Chicken & Barley

1 1/2 t. ground cumin
1 1/2 t. chili powder
1 t. salt
1 t. ground cinnamon
1 t. dried mint flakes
1 t. garlic powder
1/8 t. ground red pepper
1/8 t. black pepper
6 chicken thighs, skinned
1 T. olive oil

1 large onion, chopped
1 red bell pepper, chopped
2 T. soy sauce
1 T. sherry
3 1/2 c. chicken broth
1 1/4 c. uncooked pearl barley
1 4.5 oz. can diced tomatoes, drained
6 T. green onions, chopped

Combine the spices in a small bowl. Rub the chicken thighs with one-half of the spice mixture. Heat the olive oil in a large nonstick skillet over medium-high heat. Add the chicken; cook 1 minute on each side or until the chicken is browned. Remove the chicken from the skillet. Add the onion, bell pepper, soy sauce and sherry. Cook over medium-high heat for 3 minutes, or until the vegetables are lightly browned. Add the chicken broth, barley, tomatoes and remaining spice mixture and stir well. Add the chicken to the skillet, nestling the pieces into the vegetable mixture.

Bring to a boil; cover and reduce the heat. Simmer 45-55 minutes, or until the chicken is completely cooked through. Let stand for a few minutes before serving. Garnish with the green onions. Serves 6.

Chicken & Cheese Calzones

1 pkg. frozen bread dough, thawed and cut into fourths

1 T. extra virgin olive oil

2 c. cooked chicken breast, shredded

1/2 c. sweet onions, chopped

1/2 c. button mushrooms, cleaned and sliced

1 red bell pepper, cored, seeded and thinly sliced

2 c. prepared marinara sauce

8 oz. mozzarella cheese, grated

1/4 c. Asiago cheese, grated

1 egg, beaten

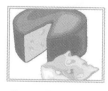

Roll each of the pieces of bread dough into an 8-inch round. Brush the bread with a bit of olive oil. Place on one half of the bread round one-fourth of the chicken, onions, mushrooms and red pepper. Carefully pour one-fourth of the marinara sauce over the chicken and vegetables and top with one-fourth of the mozzarella and Asiago cheeses. Pull the one-half of the dough over the filled half to create a half-moon-shaped calzone and seal the edges of the bread together by lightly brushing with the egg and pressing with your fingertips. Place the calzone on a baking sheet that has been coated with cooking spray. Repeat with the remaining three calzones. Bake at 350°F for 20-25 minutes, or until golden brown and cooked through. Makes 4 servings.

Chicken Scaloppini with Angel Hair Pasta

4 chicken breast halves, skinless and boneless

1/4 c. extra virgin olive oil

1 large purple onion, thinly sliced

2 cloves garlic, minced

1/2 lb. button mushrooms, thinly sliced

1 zucchini, thinly sliced

15 oz. can Italian-style stewed tomatoes

1 t. salt

1/2 t. black pepper

1/2 t. ground oregano

1 lb. angel hair pasta, cooked al dente

Place each piece of chicken breast between 2 pieces of waxed paper and pound to a uniform ¼-inch thickness. Heat the olive oil in a large skillet. Add the chicken pieces and fry for 6-8 minutes, turning once, until cooked through. Place on an ovenproof platter and keep warm in the oven. Place the onion, garlic, mushrooms, zucchini and tomatoes in the skillet and add the salt, pepper and oregano. Cover and cook over medium heat for 8-10 minutes, stirring occasionally. Add the chicken breasts and cook for 2 minutes. Serve the chicken and vegetables over the hot, cooked pasta. Serves 4-6.

Mexican Chicken Enchiladas

4 T. butter or margarine	1 t. salt
4 T. flour	10 6-inch corn tortillas
8 oz. can tomato sauce	2 c. cooked chicken, shredded
3 c. water	2 c. Pepper Jack cheese, shredded
2 T. chili powder	

 Lightly coat a 9" x 13" baking pan with cooking spray. In a medium saucepan, melt the butter over low heat. Add the flour and stir constantly until the flour and butter are thickened. Slowly add the tomato sauce, whisking until smooth. Add the water, chili powder and salt, stirring to blend well and bring to a boil. Stir over medium heat until the sauce is thickened and smooth. Wrap the corn tortillas in a paper towel and warm the tortillas in the microwave oven for 30 seconds, or until the tortillas are softened.

To assemble the enchiladas, pour enough sauce over the bottom of the baking pan to cover. Fill one tortilla with 1 heaping tablespoon of chicken and top with 1 tablespoon of cheese. Drizzle a bit of the sauce over all and wrap the tortilla tightly. Place in the baking pan, seam side down. Repeat with the remaining tortillas. Pour the remaining sauce over the chicken enchiladas and top with the remaining cheese. Cover with aluminum foil. Bake at 350°F for 30 minutes. Serves 4-5.

Italian Chicken & Sausage Rigatoni

4 chicken breast halves, cut into thin strips

1 lb. sweet Italian sausage, casings removed

1 green bell pepper, thinly sliced

1 small onion, peeled and sliced

1 large tomato, chopped

2 cloves garlic, minced

1 t. salt

1/2 t. black pepper

1/4 c. white cooking wine

1 lb. rigatoni, cooked al dente

Parmesan cheese, grated

Place the chicken and Italian sausage in a large skillet and cook and stir for 5 minutes. Remove or drain off any fat. Add the green pepper, onion, tomato, garlic, salt, pepper and wine and cook on medium heat for 5-7 minutes, or until the chicken is completely cooked and the vegetables are tender. Remove from the heat and add the rigatoni. Mix well. Top with the Parmesan cheese to serve. Serves 4-6.

Roasted Red Peppers with Turkey Stuffing

4 red bell peppers, cored and seeds removed

2 c. dry, cubed seasoned stuffing mix

1 c. boiling water

1/4 c. butter or margarine, melted

2 c. cooked turkey, finely chopped

1/2 c. walnuts, chopped

1/2 c. celery, chopped

1/4 c. onions, chopped

2 c. mozzarella cheese, shredded

 Cut each red pepper in half lengthwise and place on a baking sheet. In a medium bowl, combine the stuffing mix, boiling water and butter. Toss well. Add the cooked turkey, walnuts, celery and onions. Stuff each pepper half with the turkey and stuffing mix. Sprinkle the mozzarella cheese over each pepper. Bake, uncovered, at 350°F for 20 minutes, or until the stuffing is hot and the peppers are tender. Serves 4-6.

Southwestern Spicy Chicken Soup

2 T. vegetable oil	3 c. chicken broth
1 medium onion, chopped	1 T. chili powder
1 clove garlic, minced	1/2 t. salt
28 oz. can tomatoes, undrained	1/2 t. freshly ground black pepper
11 oz. can whole kernel corn	2 c. Jack cheese, shredded
2 c. cooked chicken, shredded	2 c. tortilla chips
4 oz. can green chilies, diced	

 Heat the oil in a large stockpot. Add the onion and garlic and cook for 2 minutes. Add the tomatoes, corn, chicken, green chilies and chicken broth and stir well. Add the chili powder, salt and pepper and mix again. Simmer, covered, for 30 minutes over low heat. To assemble the soup, place ½ cup of tortilla chips in the bottom of each of the 4 individual soup bowls. Ladle equal portions of soup into each bowl and top with the Jack cheese. Serves 4.

BBQ Smoked Chicken Pizza

12-inch prepared pizza shell (or homemade pizza dough, if desired)

1 c. prepared barbecue sauce

1/2 lb. deli-style smoked chicken, cut into thin slices

1 c. purple onion, thinly sliced

2 T. fresh parsley, finely minced

3 c. mozzarella cheese, shredded

 Place the pizza shell or prepared dough on a baking sheet that has been sprinkled with cornmeal. Heat the oven to 400°F. Spread the barbecue sauce on the pizza shell and layer the smoked chicken over the sauce. Scatter the onion rings over the chicken and sprinkle the parsley on top of the onion. Spread the mozzarella cheese over all. Bake the pizza for 12-15 minutes, or until the cheese is melted and the pizza is bubbly. Serves 6.

Mid-Winter Chicken Stew

2 T. extra virgin olive oil

1 large onion, chopped

4 chicken breast halves, boneless and skinless, cut into 1-inch cubes

6 new red potatoes, scrubbed and cut into quarters

4 carrots, peeled and cut into 1-inch pieces

14 1/2 oz. can whole tomatoes, undrained

4 ribs celery, chopped

1 t. salt

1/2 t. freshly ground black pepper

1 T. flour

1/2 c. water

 Heat the oil in a large stockpot. Add the onion and fry on medium-high heat for 2 minutes. Add the chicken and fry for 2 minutes, turning once. Add the potatoes, carrots, tomatoes, celery, salt and pepper and reduce the heat to a simmer. Simmer for 20 minutes. Combine the flour and water in a small bowl. Bring the chicken and vegetables to a boil and slowly add the flour and water, stirring until the sauce has thickened and is smooth. Reduce the heat and simmer for 2 minutes. Serves 4.

Spanish Chicken & Shrimp Paella

1/4 c. extra virgin olive oil

1 medium onion, chopped

3 cloves garlic, minced

2 T. fresh parsley, minced

pinch saffron

1 T. instant chicken bouillon granules

1 lb. chicken breasts, skinless, boneless and cut into 1-inch pieces

1 green bell pepper, thinly sliced

1 red bell pepper, thinly sliced

1 yellow bell pepper, thinly sliced

8 oz. can tomato sauce

1/2 t. sugar

4 c. long grain white rice, uncooked

7 c. water

1 t. salt

1/2 t. freshly ground black pepper

1 lb. fresh shrimp, cleaned and unpeeled with tails on

 In a large skillet, sauté the onion, garlic and parsley in the oil for 2 minutes. Add the saffron and chicken bouillon and stir. Add the chicken and pepper slices and cook over medium heat for 5 minutes. Add the tomato sauce, sugar, rice, water, salt and pepper and cover the skillet. Bring to a boil and reduce the heat to low. Cover and simmer for 10 minutes and add the shrimp. Simmer for an additional 10 minutes. Serves 6-8.

CHAPTER THREE

One-Dish Dinners Beginning with Beef

The rich and provocative flavors of beef create the perfect beginning for one-dish dinners. In this chapter, you will find a tantalizing variety of dinners using all cuts of beef and ground beef. For evenings when your family is hungry and time is short, try *Inside-Out Tacos, Hot Beef Heroes, Foil-Wrapped Sunday Dinner* or *Teriyaki Beef & Noodle Bowl.*

One-dish dinners such as *Creamy Steak & Pearl Onions, Napoleon Braciole* and *Garlic Beef & Spring Vegetables* are worthy of dinner guests, who will appreciate the flavors of beef combined with spring vegetables, herbs, garlic, onions and other fresh produce. And, when the days are short and cold, try the best of robust soups and stews, such as *Hearty Beef & Barley Soup, Shaker Valley Beef Stew* and *Angelo's Spaghetti & Meatball Soup.* Enjoy the best of beef and the best of one-dish dinners!

Inside-Out Tacos

1 lb. lean ground beef
1 medium onion
1/2 t. chili powder
6 6-inch corn tortillas, cut into small pieces
1 1/2 c. cheddar cheese, grated
1 c. prepared salsa

10 3/4 oz. can condensed tomato soup
1/4 c. water
1/4 c. milk
lettuce, shredded
tomatoes, chopped
dairy sour cream

Brown the ground beef in a large sauté pan and drain the excess fat. Add the onion and chili powder and cook for 2 minutes. Lightly coat a 2 quart baking pan with cooking spray. Layer half of the tortilla pieces in the bottom of the pan and spoon the beef and onions over the tortillas. Sprinkle one-half of the cheese over the beef and onions. Layer the remaining tortilla pieces over the cheese. Combine the salsa, tomato soup, water and milk in a medium bowl. Pour the sauce over the beef and tortillas. Sprinkle the remaining cheese over the top of the sauce. Cover with aluminum foil and bake at 400°F for 30 minutes, or until heated through and bubbly. To serve, pass the lettuce, tomatoes and sour cream as toppings. Serves 4-6.

Sirloin Pepper Steak

1 lb. beef boneless sirloin tip
   steak (slightly frozen)

1 T. vegetable oil

1 medium onion, sliced into rings

1 clove garlic, minced

1 green bell pepper, cored and
   sliced into rings

2 T. soy sauce

1 t. honey

1 t. five-spice powder

1/2 t. black pepper

1 T. cornstarch

1 T. water

6 c. hot, cooked rice

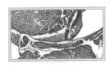

Remove any visible fat and cut the sirloin steak across the grain in thin slices about 1-inch in length. Heat the oil in a large sauté pan and add the steak strips. Fry for 1 minute. Add the onion, garlic and green pepper and cook for 2 minutes. In a small bowl, combine the soy sauce, honey, five-spice powder, black pepper, cornstarch and water and whisk until well-combined. Add the sauce to the sauté pan and heat to boiling, stirring constantly. Reduce the heat and cook for 2 minutes. Serve hot over the rice. Serves 4.

Chili & Cornbread Bake

1 lb. lean ground beef

1 small onion, chopped

1 clove garlic, minced

15 oz. can chili beans, reserve 1/4 c. liquid

11 oz. can Mexican corn, drained

2 T. chili powder

1/2 t. black pepper

1 T. flour

1 c. prepared baking mix

1/2 c. canned creamed corn

1/2 c. yellow cornmeal

1 egg, beaten

1 T. sugar

1 c. milk

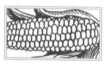

Brown the ground beef in a large skillet and drain any excess fat. Add the onion and garlic and cook for 2 minutes over medium heat. Add the chili beans, corn, chili powder and black pepper and mix well. Mix together the reserved bean liquid and the flour in a small cup and add to the chili mixture. Heat to boiling and cook on medium heat for 2 minutes. Lightly coat a 9" x 13" baking pan with cooking spray and spread the beef and beans in the bottom of the pan.

In a medium mixing bowl, combine the baking mix, creamed corn, cornmeal, egg, sugar and milk. Beat to form a soft batter. Turn the batter over the chili mix and spread evenly in the pan. Bake at 350°F for 55-60 minutes, or until the cornbread and chili are cooked through and bubbly. Serves 8.

London Pub Beef & Potato Fry

4 medium potatoes	1 t. freshly ground black pepper
1 lb. beef London broil steak (slightly frozen)	1/2 t. garlic salt
4 T. vegetable oil, divided	10 oz. pkg. frozen French-cut green beans, thawed and drained
1 medium onion, chopped	

 Scrub the potatoes and cut a thin slit in the top of each. Microwave the potatoes for 10 minutes, or until tender. Cool and slice in ¼-inch thick slices. Meanwhile, remove any visible fat from the London broil. Cut thin slices across the grain about 2-inches in length. Heat 2 tablespoons of the oil in a large skillet over medium-high heat. Add the onion and fry for 1 minute. Add the beef, pepper and garlic salt and fry for 2 minutes. Remove the beef and onions from the pan and set aside.

Heat the remaining oil in the pan and add the potatoes. Fry over medium-high heat for 5 minutes. Add the beef mixture and the green beans. Cover and cook over medium heat until the beans are heated through, about 3 minutes. Serves 4.

Shaker Valley Beef Stew

3 lbs. boneless chuck or round beef, cut into 1-inch cubes

1/2 c. flour

2 t. salt

1 t. black pepper

1/4 c. butter or margarine

1 bay leaf

1 t. dried thyme

2 T. fresh parsley, minced

1 t. salt

1/2 t. black pepper

3 c. water

1 lb. small onions, peeled and cut in half

1 lb. baby carrots, cleaned

10 new red potatoes, scrubbed and cut in half

1/4 c. flour

1/4 c. water

5 ribs celery, cut in 1-inch pieces

2 c. prepared baking mix

1/2 c. cheddar cheese, shredded

1 egg

1/2 c. milk

Combine the flour, salt and pepper and dredge the beef cubes thoroughly in the mixture. Heat the butter in a large skillet or stockpot and brown the beef on all sides. Remove the beef when browned. When all the beef is browned, return it to the pot and add the bay leaf, thyme, parsley, salt and pepper. Mix well with the pan drippings. Add the water, cover and heat to boiling. Reduce the heat and simmer for 2 hours. Add the onions, carrots and potatoes and continue cooking for 15 minutes. Bring the stew to a boil and combine the flour and water in a small bowl. Add to the boiling stew and stir until the sauce is thickened and smooth.

Make the dumplings by combining the baking mix, cheddar cheese, egg and milk in a medium bowl. Mix just until the ingredients are moistened. Drop the dumplings onto the top of the meat or vegetable pieces, using 1 large tablespoon of dough per dumpling. Cover and cook for 10 minutes. To serve, remove the cooked dumplings and spoon the stew into bowls. Replace the dumplings on each individual serving. Serves 8.

Hong Kong Stir-Fry Beef

1 1/2 lbs. beef round steak
(partially frozen)

1/4 c. vegetable oil

1 small onion, sliced

1 1/2 c. celery, cut in thin
diagonal slices

1 c. carrots, cut in thin diagonal
slices

1 T. cornstarch

1/4 c. soy sauce

8 oz. can tomato sauce

1 t. sugar

1/4 t. ginger

1 green bell pepper, cut in strips

1/2 c. fresh mushrooms, thinly
sliced

1/2 c. water chestnuts, thinly
sliced

6 c. hot, cooked rice

Cut the steak into thin strips about 2-inches in length. Heat the oil a large skillet or wok and fry the steak for 2 minutes. Add the onion, celery and carrots and fry until tender-crisp, about 4 minutes. In a small bowl, combine the cornstarch, soy sauce, tomato sauce, sugar and ginger. Add the sauce to the skillet and heat through. Add the green pepper, mushrooms and water chestnuts. Cook and stir for 3-4 minutes, or until the sauce is thickened and the vegetables are heated. Serve over hot rice. Serves 4.

Hot Beef Heroes

6 slices bacon
1 lb. beef ground chuck
1 onion, chopped
1/2 c. ripe olives, chopped
1/4 c. catsup
1 T. Dijon mustard
1/2 t. salt

1 t. chili powder
6 slices American cheese
6 slices cheddar cheese
6 large hero or sandwich buns, split
Parmesan cheese for garnish

 Fry the bacon in a large skillet until brown. Remove and drain on paper towels. Crumble the bacon and set aside. Place the ground beef in the skillet and brown. Drain any excess fat. Add the onion, olives, catsup, mustard, salt and chili powder and cook for 2 minutes.

Assemble the sandwiches by placing 1 hero bun on a square of aluminum foil about 8" x 8" in size. Open the bun and place 1 slice each of the American and cheddar cheese on 1 side of the bun. Scoop 2 tablespoons of the meat mixture and spread on the other side of the bun. Sprinkle the bacon crumbles over the meat. Wrap the sandwich securely in the foil and repeat the process with the remaining buns. Bake the sandwiches at 375°F for 10 minutes and serve immediately. Serves 6.

Napoleon Braciole

4 thin slices top round beef, (about 10" x 3" x 1/4")	1 T. extra virgin olive oil
1/4 c. dry Italian-seasoned bread crumbs	1 T. flour
	1 T. butter or margarine
2/3 c. dry red wine	1/2 c. water
1/4 c. beef salami, finely chopped	1 T. tomato paste
1/2 c. Parmesan cheese, grated	1/2 t. salt
1/2 t. dried oregano	1/4 t. freshly ground black pepper

 Place each piece of beef between 2 sheets of waxed paper and pound with a meat mallet until very thin (about 1/8-inch thickness). Sprinkle 1 tablespoon of bread crumbs and 2 tablespoons of red wine over each piece of beef. Scatter equal portions of the salami, cheese and oregano over each piece of beef. Roll each piece of beef tightly and tie with cooking string or secure with toothpicks. Heat the oil in a large skillet and fry the rolls for 8 minutes, turning each roll once. Remove the beef from the pan.

Combine the flour and butter in the skillet and stir while heating. Add the water gradually. Add the tomato paste, salt and pepper and heat until thickened and smooth. Replace the beef rolls in the skillet with the sauce and simmer for 10-15 minutes, or until the meat is tender and cooked through. To serve, remove the string or toothpicks and cut the rolls into slices about ½-inch thick. Serve over noodles or rice, spooning the remaining sauce over the top. Serves 4-6.

Touchdown Beef Chili

1 lb. lean ground beef

1 medium onion, chopped

1 t. garlic powder

15 oz. can red kidney beans, undrained

15 oz. can chili beans

28 oz. can crushed tomatoes, undrained

1/2 c. green bell pepper, diced (optional)

8 oz. can tomato sauce

2 T. chili powder

1 c. cheddar cheese, shredded

 Brown the ground beef in a large saucepan. Drain any excess fat. Add the onion and garlic powder and cook for 1 minute. Add the kidney beans, chili beans, tomatoes, bell pepper (if using), tomato sauce, and the chili powder. Mix well to combine. Cook, covered, over medium heat for 25-30 minutes, or until the flavors are well-combined. To serve, ladle into bowls and top with the shredded cheese. Serves 4-6.

Hearty Beef Stroganoff

2 T. vegetable oil

1 c. onions, chopped

1 1/2 lbs. boneless top sirloin
steak, cut into thin strips

1 t. freshly ground black pepper

10 3/4 oz. can cream of
mushroom soup

1/4 c. half and half cream

1 c. dairy sour cream

1 lb. wide egg noodles, cooked al
dente

parsley for garnish

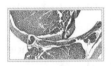 Heat the oil in a large skillet and add the onions. Cook over medium-high heat for 2 minutes. Reduce the heat to medium and add the steak strips. Sprinkle with the black pepper. Cook for 3-4 minutes, or until the beef is no longer pink. Mix together in a small bowl, the cream of mushroom soup, half and half cream and the sour cream. Reduce the heat to low and slowly add the stroganoff sauce, mixing the sauce with the beef and onions. Simmer for 3-4 minutes. Serve immediately over the hot egg noodles and garnish with the parsley. Serves 4-6.

Foil-Wrapped Sunday Beef Dinner

3 lbs. beef chuck roast

3 large russet potatoes, cut into quarters

3 large carrots, peeled and cut into 2-inch pieces

1 large onion, peeled and cut into quarters

1 1/2 oz. pkg. dry onion soup mix

10 3/4 oz. can cream of mushroom soup

2 T. water

 Cut 2 large pieces of aluminum foil to overlap a 9" x 13" baking pan. Tightly seal any cut edges in the pan. Place the roast in the middle of the foil. Add the potatoes, carrots and onion around and on top of the roast. In a small bowl, mix together the onion soup mix and cream of mushroom soup. Spoon the sauce over the roast and vegetables and sprinkle the water over all. Cut 2 pieces of aluminum foil and tightly seal the top of the roast and vegetables, tucking and sealing in all of the edges. Bake at 325°F for 3 hours, or until the meat and vegetables are very tender. Serve, spooning the gravy over the meat and vegetables. Serves 4-6.

Garlic Beef & Spring Vegetables

5-6 lbs. beef rump roast

16 cloves garlic, thinly sliced

1/4 c. extra virgin olive oil

4 carrots, peeled and cut into matchstick pieces

4 russet potatoes, peeled and cut into small chunks

4 large tomatoes, cut into quarters

1 large sweet onion, sliced into rings and separated

1 T. fresh oregano, chopped

1 T. fresh parsley, chopped

1 T. fresh rosemary, chopped

2 t. freshly ground black pepper

1 t. salt

2 c. hot water

 Cut very thin pockets all over the roast and insert the garlic slices into each pocket. Heat the oil in a large stockpot or skillet and brown the roast in the oil for 2-3 minutes, turning to brown evenly. Add the carrots, potatoes, tomatoes and onion and stir to mix the vegetables around the roast. Sprinkle the oregano, parsley, rosemary, pepper and salt over the roast and vegetables and pour the water over all. Cover tightly and simmer for 1½ to 2 hours, or until the meat is very tender and the vegetables are cooked through. To serve, slice the roast and serve with equal portions of the vegetables. Serves 4-6.

Malaysian Beef Curry

2 lbs. boneless beef chuck roast	2 stalks lemongrass, chopped
2 T. sesame oil	4 c. water
2 medium onions, chopped	2 T. lemon juice
3 T. soy sauce	1/4 t. ground cinnamon
1 T. cornstarch	1/4 c. black bean garlic sauce
1 t. crushed red chili peppers	6 c. hot, cooked jasmine rice

Heat the oil in a large pan over medium-high heat. Add the roast and brown on all sides for about 4 minutes. Remove the meat from the pan and add the onions. Cook the onions on medium heat for 4 minutes. Combine the soy sauce and cornstarch in a small bowl and add to the onions. Mix well. Add the chili peppers. Return the roast to the pan and arrange the lemongrass around the beef. Pour the water over the roast and add the lemon juice and cinnamon. Simmer over low heat for 1½ hours, or until the meat is tender. Add the garlic sauce and stir to combine. Shred the roast in small pieces and return to the sauce. To serve, ladle the roast and sauce over individual bowls of hot rice. Serves 6.

Peppered Roast Beef

3-4 lbs. beef cross-rib or rump roast

2 T. freshly ground black pepper

1 T. garlic powder

3 medium onions, cut into quarters

6 small potatoes, cut into quarters

6 carrots, peeled and cut in 2-inch pieces

1 bay leaf

 Rub the roast with the black pepper, covering as much of the roast as possible. Dust the roast with the garlic powder. Place the roast in a 9" x 13" baking pan. Place the onions, potatoes and carrots around the roast and add the bay leaf. Cover tightly with aluminum foil and bake at 325°F for 2½ to 3 hours, or until the meat is tender. Slice the beef to serve with the vegetables. Serves 4.

Slow-Roasted Beef Brisket with Spicy Mustard Sauce

3 lbs. beef brisket
6 c. water
1/4 c. fresh parsley, chopped
6 ribs celery, cut in 1-inch pieces
6 carrots, cut in 1-inch pieces
3 onions, roughly chopped
1 t. salt
1 t. freshly ground black pepper
1 t. dried thyme
1/2 t. dried rosemary
1 bay leaf

Spicy Mustard Sauce:
1/4 c. flour
1/2 c. half and half cream
1/2 c. Dijon mustard
1 t. Worcestershire sauce
1/2 t. black pepper

Place the beef in a large stockpot or deep skillet. Cover with the water and add the parsley, celery, carrots, onions, salt, pepper, thyme, rosemary and bay leaf. Stir and cover. Simmer for 3 hours, or until the beef is tender. Remove the brisket and place on a platter with the vegetables. Remove the bay leaf. Reserve the remaining broth in the pan to prepare the sauce.

To make the sauce, heat the broth to boiling and whisk in the flour. Stir until the sauce is thickened and smooth. Gradually add the cream and stir well. Add the Dijon mustard and blend again. Add the Worcestershire sauce and pepper. Serve the brisket with the vegetables and pour the sauce over all. Serves 6.

Creamy Steak & Pearl Onions

1 lb. beef sirloin steak, cut into
   1-inch slices

2 T. extra virgin olive oil

1/2 t. salt

1/2 t. freshly ground black pepper

2 c. half and half cream

3 oz. cream cheese

3 T. canned tomato paste

4 oz. can mushrooms, sliced

1 c. frozen pearl onions, thawed
   and drained

8 oz. wide egg noodles, cooked al
   dente

Heat the oil in a large skillet and add the steak strips. Fry for 2 minutes. Season with the salt and pepper. Stir in the cream, cream cheese and tomato paste and blend well. Cook for 1 minute over medium-low heat. Add the mushrooms and onions and mix. Cook for 3-4 minutes over medium-low heat. Serve the beef and vegetables over the hot, cooked egg noodles. Serves 4.

Hearty Beef & Barley Soup

1 lb. beef stew meat, cut into small chunks

2 T. extra virgin olive oil

8 c. water

2 T. instant beef bouillon granules

1 t. salt

1 t. black pepper

2 cloves garlic, minced

2 ribs celery, sliced

1/2 c. pearl barley

4 carrots, peeled and cubed

1 sweet onion, chopped

1 c. frozen chopped spinach, thawed

 Brown the meat in the olive oil in a large stockpot. Turn and cook for 2 minutes. Add the water, beef bouillon, salt, pepper and garlic and simmer for 1½ hours. Stir and add the celery, barley, carrots and onion and simmer for 20 minutes. Add the spinach and simmer for 5 minutes. Serves 4.

Russian Beef Borscht

1 lb. beef chuck roast, cut into
  small pieces
1 T. vegetable oil
8 c. beef broth
1 t. salt
1/2 t. black pepper
2 bay leaves

8 oz. can tomato sauce
1 head green cabbage, shredded
6 carrots, peeled and chopped
1 yellow onion, chopped
16 oz. can beets, cut in julienne
  pieces, drained
sour cream for garnish

 Sear the beef cubes in the oil in a large stockpot. Fry for 2 minutes. Add the beef broth, salt, pepper and bay leaves and simmer for 1 hour. Remove the bay leaves and add the tomato sauce, cabbage, carrots and onion. Stir to mix well and simmer for 40 minutes. Add the beets and simmer for 5 minutes. To serve, ladle the soup into individual bowls and add a dollop of sour cream to each. Serves 6.

Angelo's Spaghetti & Meatball Soup

1/2 lb. ground veal	6 oz. can tomato paste
1/2 lb. ground beef	8 oz. jar sliced mushrooms
1 c. seasoned bread crumbs	1 bay leaf
1 large onion, chopped, divided	1 t. salt
2 cloves garlic, minced	1 t. freshly ground black pepper
1/2 t. dried Italian seasoning	4 oz. spaghetti, broken in 2-inch pieces
8 c. chicken broth	
2 28 oz. cans crushed tomatoes	Parmesan cheese for garnish

 Prepare the meatballs by combining the veal, beef, bread crumbs, 1 tablespoon onion, garlic and Italian seasoning. Mix lightly with your hands and form into 24 meatballs. Refrigerate for 30 minutes.

In a large stockpot, combine the chicken broth, remaining onion, tomatoes, tomato paste, mushrooms, bay leaf, salt and pepper. Add the meatballs, cover and cook on medium-low heat for 50-60 minutes, or until the meatballs are cooked through. Add the dry spaghetti noodles and cook for 15 minutes over medium heat until the noodles are cooked al dente. Sprinkle the Parmesan cheese over the soup to serve. Serves 6.

Sloppy Joe Meat Pies

1 lb. lean ground beef	1/2 c. catsup
2 T. canned green chilies, chopped	1 T. brown sugar
1/4 c. onion, chopped	1 t. prepared mustard
1 t. salt	1/4 c. dairy sour cream
1/2 t. pepper	10 extra-large refrigerated biscuits

 Brown the ground beef and drain any excess fat. Add the green chilies, onion, salt, pepper, catsup, brown sugar and mustard and blend well. Cook on medium heat for 3 minutes. Reduce the heat to low and add the sour cream, mixing again. On a flat surface, roll each biscuit to a 6-inch circle. Place a heaping tablespoon of the sloppy Joe mix on one-half of the biscuit and cover with the other half to form a half-circle. Crimp the edges of the pie with a fork to seal and place on a baking sheet. Repeat with the remaining biscuits. Bake the pies at 375°F for 15-20 minutes, or until cooked through and hot. Serves 5.

Asian Broccoli & Beef

1 lb. boneless top sirloin steak	1/2 c. water
2 T. sesame oil	1 t. ground ginger
1 clove garlic, minced	2 c. fresh broccoli, cut into small florets
1/4 c. soy sauce	
2 T. cornstarch	6 c. hot, cooked brown rice
	2 T. toasted sesame seeds

 Cut the steak across the grain of the meat in thin slices about 2 inches in length. Heat the oil in a large sauté pan or skillet and add the beef and garlic. In a small bowl, combine the soy sauce, cornstarch, water and ginger and pour over the beef. Heat to a boil, reduce the heat to low and simmer for 3-4 minutes. Stir to blend and thicken the sauce. Add the broccoli and simmer, covered, for 10 minutes, or until the broccoli is tender-crisp. To serve, arrange the beef and broccoli over the rice and cover with the sauce. Top with the toasted sesame seeds. Serves 4.

Thornley's Cornish Pasties

4 small potatoes, peeled and cut into thin slices

1 lb. beef top round steak, cut into very small cubes

1 c. onion, chopped

1/4 c. fresh parsley, minced

1/4 c. butter or margarine

salt and pepper to taste

Pastry:

1 1/3 c. vegetable shortening

2 t. salt

3/4 c. water

4 c. flour

Make the pastry by combining the shortening with the salt in a large mixing bowl. Add the water and 1 cup of flour. Use the electric mixer to slowly blend and add the remaining flour, 1 cup at a time until the dough is smooth. Divide the dough into 4 equal portions. Lightly flour a large piece of waxed paper and roll one piece of the pastry into an oval 8" x 10" shape.

Assemble the pasties by layering one-fourth of the potatoes, one-fourth of the beef and one-fourth of the onions in a long, narrow oval shape to fit the pastry. Generously sprinkle the pasties with salt and pepper. Top with one-fourth of the parsley and dot with one-fourth of the butter. Close the pastie by folding the two longest edges of the pastie together and slowly pull the waxed paper away. Crimp the edges of the pastry across the top and on the sides and press slightly into a crescent shape. Pierce the pastry with a fork in 2 or 3 places. Place on a baking sheet that has been lightly coated with cooking spray. Repeat with the remaining pasties. Bake at 450°F for 15 minutes. Reduce the heat to 350°F and bake for 30 minutes, or until the pasties are hot and cooked through. Serve with malt vinegar, if desired. Makes 4 large pasties.

Teriyaki Beef & Noodle Bowl

1 lb. beef top sirloin steak (partially frozen)

1 T. sesame oil

15 oz. can beef broth

1 clove garlic, minced

1/2 c. prepared teriyaki sauce

2 green onions, thinly sliced

1 carrot, peeled and cut in thin 1-inch matchsticks

1 c. mushrooms, cut in thin slices

1 c. fresh bean sprouts, cleaned and cut into 1-inch pieces

1/2 lb. Japanese udon noodles, cooked and drained

Cut the steak across the grain into very thin matchstick strips about 1-inch in length. Using a large saucepan or skillet, heat the beef in the oil over medium heat for 2 minutes. Add the beef broth, garlic and teriyaki sauce and cook and stir for 2 minutes. Add the green onions, carrot and mushrooms and cook for 2 minutes. Add the bean sprouts and the noodles and mix well over medium-low heat until the meat, noodles and vegetables are all heated through. Serve immediately. Serves 4.

Texas-Style BBQ Roast & Red Rice

3 lbs. beef chuck roast	1/2 c. catsup
1/2 c. brown sugar	1/4 c. chili sauce
2 c. prepared barbecue sauce	8 c. hot, cooked long grain white rice

Place the roast in a large baking pan and cover with foil. Bake at 350°F for 1 hour. Drain the juices and discard. Cover the roast with a thin layer of brown sugar. In a small bowl, combine the barbecue sauce, catsup and chili sauce and pour over the roast. Bake, uncovered, at 325°F for 2 hours, basting occasionally with the sauce. To serve, pour the sauce over the hot rice and top with the roast beef. Serves 6-8.

Chinese Beef Short Ribs

1 large onion, sliced	1 clove garlic, minced
2 T. sesame oil	1 lb. small whole carrots
3 lbs. beef short ribs	1/4 c. soy sauce
1 t. ginger	1/4 c. white cooking wine
2 T. sugar	1/2 c. beef broth
1 t. salt	6 c. hot, cooked jasmine rice
1/2 t. black pepper	

 Sauté the onion in the sesame oil in a large stockpot or Dutch oven. Add the short ribs and brown on medium-high heat for 2-3 minutes, turning once. Add the ginger, sugar, salt, pepper, garlic, carrots, soy sauce, wine and beef broth and mix well. Simmer over medium-low heat for 2 hours, or until the ribs are tender. Remove the bones from the ribs and return the meat to the sauce and vegetables. Serve over the hot rice. Serves 6.

CHAPTER FOUR

One-Dish Dinners Beginning with Pork & Lamb

Whether you use ham, pork, or lamb, the distinctive flavors of these meats create delectable one-dish dinners. The herbs and spices that are used with these meats also take on a new importance, as they complement and contrast with the meat. Lamb carries the freshness of rosemary and garlic in delicious dinners. Pork is particularly enhanced by citrus flavors and sweet accompaniments. Ham is bold and can be partnered quite well with creamy sauces and pasta.

In this chapter, several one-dish dinners use pasta and rice as a basis. Try *Prosciutto & Walnut Pesto Pasta, Smoked Ham & Mushroom Risotto* or *Pasta a la Carbonara.* One-dish dinners that were created in the far corners of the earth are also tempting — *Greek Lamb Skillet, Latino Lamb Ribs, Pork Chili Verde* and *Caribbean Pork Sausage & Rice.* You will find here recipes that are familiar and comforting, as well as many that are new — try them all for delightful one-dish dinners!

Pasta a la Carbonara

1/4 lb. salt pork (you may use
    1/4 lb. bacon, if desired)
10 c. water
1 t. salt
1 lb. spaghetti, broken in half

2 eggs, beaten
1 c. frozen peas, thawed
salt and pepper to taste
1/4 c. freshly grated Parmesan
    cheese

Cut the salt pork into small cubes and fry over medium-high heat in a sauté pan until well-browned, about 4 minutes. Set aside. In a large stockpot, heat the water to a boil and add the salt. Cook the spaghetti noodles in the boiling water until they are al dente. Drain and set aside. Place a large, heatproof serving bowl on top of the stockpot, allowing the hot stockpot to heat the serving bowl. Pour the eggs into the serving bowl and mix with the spaghetti, peas and salt pork or bacon. Working quickly, toss to combine, season with salt and pepper to taste and add the Parmesan cheese. Toss again. Serve immediately. Serves 4.

Caribbean Pork Sausage & Rice

1 lb. spicy pork link sausages	6 oz. can tomato paste
1/2 c. cooked ham, chopped	2 1/2 c. water
1 onion, chopped	1 t. salt
1 green bell pepper, chopped	1/2 t. ground oregano
1 clove garlic, minced	1 c. long grain white rice, uncooked

 Brown the sausages in a large skillet or sauté pan for 2-3 minutes, turning to brown evenly. Add the ham, onion, green pepper and garlic. Cook and stir over medium heat for 2 minutes. Add the tomato paste, water, salt and oregano. Heat to boiling and add the rice. Reduce the heat and simmer on low for 20-25 minutes, or until the rice is tender. Serves 6.

Parmesan Ham & Potato Bake

10 3/4 oz. can condensed cream of mushroom soup

1/2 c. half and half cream

1/2 t. black pepper

4 baking potatoes, peeled and thinly sliced

2 c. fully cooked ham, chopped

1 large onion, peeled and thinly sliced

1/2 c. Parmesan cheese, grated

 In a small bowl, combine the soup, cream and black pepper, stirring to blend well. Coat a 3 quart baking dish with cooking spray. Layer one-half of the potatoes with one-half of the ham and one-half of the onion slices. Pour one-half of the soup mixture over the onion slices. Repeat the layers again. Cover and bake at 375°F for 1 hour. Uncover, sprinkle with the Parmesan cheese and continue baking for 15 minutes. Serves 6-8.

Pork Loin Chops in Tomato Ragout

4 pork loin chops, 1-inch thick	1 green bell pepper, sliced
1 T. extra virgin olive oil	2 c. beef broth
1 c. long grain white rice, uncooked	1/4 t. dried marjoram
	1/4 t. dried thyme
1 large onion, sliced	1 t. salt
3 large, ripe tomatoes, sliced	1/2 t. black pepper

Brown the pork chops in the oil in a sauté pan for 2 minutes on each side. Set aside. Coat a large baking pan with cooking spray and spread the rice on the bottom of the pan. Layer the onion, tomatoes, green pepper and pork chops over the rice. Combine the beef broth with the herbs, salt and pepper and pour over the chops and vegetables. Cover tightly and bake at 350°F for 1 hour. Serves 4.

Pork & Vegetable Pilaf

4 pork loin chops, 1-inch thick   1/2 c. red bell peppers, chopped
1 t. lemon pepper   15 oz. can chicken broth
1 T. extra virgin olive oil   1/4 c. walnuts, chopped
1/2 c. broccoli florets   2 c. uncooked instant brown rice
1/2 c. whole baby carrots   soy sauce to taste
1/2 c. mushrooms, sliced

In a large skillet, sauté the pork chops in the oil, seasoning with the lemon pepper while cooking. Cook over medium heat for 5 minutes. Turn and cook for 5 minutes. Remove the chops and set aside. Place the broccoli, carrots, mushrooms, red peppers, broth and walnuts in the same pan and bring to a boil. Add the rice and the soy sauce and reduce the heat to low. Cover and simmer for 6-8 minutes, or until the rice is done. Return the pork chops to the pan and cover again, heating for 2 minutes. Serves 4.

Pork & Mushroom Bok Choy

1 lb. lean ground pork	2 zucchini, thinly sliced
1 t. vegetable oil	1 c. water chestnuts, sliced
1 c. long grain white rice, uncooked	2 c. Chinese bok choy, torn into small pieces
8 shiitake mushrooms, sliced	1/4 c. dark soy sauce
1 small onion, chopped	1 t. ground ginger
3 carrots, peeled and cut into cubes	1/2 t. freshly ground black pepper
	2 c. chicken broth

Brown the pork in the oil in a large wok or skillet. Break up the pork and drain any excess fat. Add the rice, mushrooms, onion, carrots, zucchini, water chestnuts and bok choy. Mix lightly. In a small bowl, combine the soy sauce, ginger and pepper and pour over the vegetables and pork. Pour the chicken broth over all. Cook over low heat to simmer the vegetables and cook the rice for 20-25 minutes. Serves 4.

Angel's Camp Quiche

3 c. russet potatoes, mashed
1 T. fresh parsley, minced
2 green onions, finely sliced
5 eggs, separated
1 c. cooked ham, finely diced

1 c. cheddar cheese, shredded
1 1/4 c. milk
1/2 c. Parmesan cheese, grated
 salt and pepper to taste

 In a medium bowl, combine the potatoes, parsley and onions. Add the salt and pepper to taste. Beat one egg and add to the potato and vegetables. Lightly coat a 10-inch pie pan with cooking spray. Make a crust by pressing the potato mixture into the bottom and sides of the pan. Sprinkle the ham and cheddar cheese over the potatoes. Beat the remaining 4 eggs until well combined. Add the milk and beat again. Gently pour the egg/milk mixture over the quiche. Sprinkle Parmesan cheese over the top of the quiche and bake at 350°F for 45-55 minutes, or until the quiche is set. Allow the quiche to stand for 10 minutes before serving. Serves 6.

Sweet & Sour Pork

2 T. peanut oil

2 cloves garlic, minced

3 carrots, peeled and sliced

1 onion, peeled and roughly cut into large pieces

1 lb. boneless pork, cut into 1-inch pieces

1 green bell pepper, roughly cut into large pieces

15 1/4 oz. can pineapple chunks packed in juice

2 T. rice wine vinegar

1 t. ground ginger

2 T. soy sauce

2 T. cornstarch

2 T. water

6 c. hot, cooked rice

 Heat the oil in a large skillet or wok and add the garlic. Fry for 1 minute. Add the carrots, onion, and pork and cook over medium heat for 4-5 minutes. Add the green pepper and pineapple chunks, reserving the pineapple liquid. Cook for 2 minutes. In a small bowl, combine the juice, vinegar, ginger and soy sauce and mix well. Add to the pork and vegetables and cook for 1 minute. In a small cup, combine the cornstarch and water and stir to dissolve. Heat the pork and vegetables to a boil and quickly stir in the cornstarch and water, stirring until the sauce is smooth and blended. Serve immediately over the rice. Serves 4.

Ham 'N' Cheddar Bake

2 c. fully cooked ham, chopped

3 c. macaroni pasta, cooked and drained

1 c. fresh broccoli, cut into small florets

1/2 c. cheddar cheese, shredded

3 green onions, thinly sliced

10 3/4 oz. condensed cheddar cheese soup

1/4 c. milk

1/2 t. black pepper

1 c. potato chips, crushed

 Lightly coat a 2 quart baking dish with cooking spray. In a large bowl, combine the ham, pasta, broccoli, cheddar cheese and green onions. Blend the soup and milk in a small bowl and add to the ham and vegetables. Sprinkle with black pepper and top with the potato chips. Cover and bake at 350°F for 30 minutes. Uncover and bake for 10 minutes. Serves 6.

Greek Lamb Skillet

1/2 lb. ground lamb	2 c. frozen cut green beans
1/2 c. onion, chopped	1/4 c. tomato sauce
1 clove garlic, minced	1/2 t. ground oregano
15 oz. can beef broth	1/4 t. ground cinnamon
1 1/2 c. penne pasta, uncooked	1/2 c. feta cheese, crumbled
15 oz. can diced tomatoes	

 Brown the ground lamb in a skillet or large sauté pan. Add the onion and garlic and cook for 3 minutes. Drain any excess fat. Add the beef broth and bring to a boil. Add the pasta and simmer, covered, for 7-8 minutes, or until the pasta is almost completely cooked. Add the tomatoes, green beans, tomato sauce, oregano and cinnamon and cook over low heat until the vegetables are heated through and the spices are absorbed. Sprinkle the feta cheese just before serving. Serves 4.

Italian Sausage Rigatoni

1 T. extra virgin olive oil	2 c. crushed Italian-style tomatoes
1 lb. andouille sausage, casings removed	1 t. salt
	1/2 t. freshly ground black pepper
2 cloves garlic	1 lb. rigatoni, cooked al dente
1 large onion, chopped	1/4 lb. mozzarella cheese, shredded
1 green bell pepper, chopped	

Heat the oil in a large sauté pan and add the sausage. Cook and crumble over medium heat until browned. Add the garlic and onion and fry for 2 minutes. Add the green pepper, tomatoes, salt and pepper and cook for 10 minutes, or until the green pepper is tender and the tomatoes are cooked through. Remove from the heat and add the rigatoni. Toss to combine. Top with the mozzarella cheese and serve immediately. Serves 4.

Latino Lamb Ribs

1 T. extra virgin olive oil	1/2 t. black pepper
2 lbs. lamb riblets	4 c. chicken broth
2 c. long grain white rice	4 oz. can green chilies, diced
1/2 t. ground cumin	1/2 c. white onion, chopped
1 t. ground chili powder	11 oz. can whole kernel corn, drained
1/2 t. salt	

Heat the olive oil in a large skillet or sauté pan and add the lamb. Brown the lamb on all sides, turning occasionally for 5-6 minutes. Set aside. Add the rice, cumin, chili powder, salt and pepper and stir to coat the rice well. Add the chicken broth to the skillet and stir to remove the bits of lamb from the bottom of the pan. Add the green chilies, onion and corn and stir again. Heat to boiling and reduce the heat to low. Add the lamb and cover. Simmer for 20-25 minutes, or until the rice has absorbed the broth and is tender. Serves 4-6.

Polish Sausage & Potato Skillet

2 T. vegetable oil

4 large potatoes, peeled and cubed

1 lb. cooked Polish kielbasa, cut into 1/2-inch thick slices

1 onion, sliced

1 t. salt

1/2 t. freshly ground black pepper

1 c. frozen green peas, thawed and drained

 Heat the oil in a large sauté pan and add the potatoes. Cook over medium-high heat for 5 minutes, or until browned. Turn once. Add the sausage and onion and continue cooking for 2 minutes. Sprinkle the sausage and onions with the salt and pepper and add the green peas. Cook for 2-3 minutes and serve immediately. Serves 4.

Irish Supper Soup

1 lb. smoked ham, chopped

1 T. vegetable oil

6 baking potatoes, peeled and cut into cubes

2 large onions, thinly sliced

1 carrot, peeled and grated

10 c. beef broth

2 c. water

2 t. salt

1 t. black pepper

1/2 head cabbage, shredded

1/2 c. fresh parsley, chopped

Place the ham in a large stockpot and add the oil. Heat to medium and cook for 2 minutes. Add the potatoes and cook for 2 minutes. Add the onions, carrot, beef broth, water, salt and pepper and simmer for 45 minutes, covered. Add the cabbage and parsley and simmer for 10 minutes. Serves 4.

Favorite Split Pea Soup

1 lb. dried green split peas	1/2 t. dried rosemary
1 lb. baked ham	4 ribs celery, sliced
8 c. water	2 c. carrots, chopped
1 bay leaf	1/4 c. parsley, minced
2 onions, chopped	1 t. salt
1 t. dried marjoram	1/2 t. black pepper
1/2 t. dried thyme	

 Sort the peas and discard any debris. Place the peas, ham, water and bay leaf in a large stockpot and heat to a boil. Remove any foam and reduce the heat to a simmer. Add the onions, cover, and simmer for 1 hour. Add the marjoram, thyme, rosemary, celery, carrots, parsley, salt and pepper and simmer for 30-45 minutes, or until the peas are very tender. Remove the bay leaf and ham from the soup. Puree one-half of the soup in a blender. Return the soup to the stockpot. Cut the ham into small pieces and return to the stockpot. Discard the bay leaf. Heat and stir the soup until warmed through again. Serves 6.

Rainy Day Pork 'N' Beans

4 slices bacon

3 16 oz. cans pork and beans

2 beef wieners, cut into 1-inch
pieces

1/2 c. catsup

2 T. tomato sauce

1/2 c. onion, chopped

2 T. honey

1 T. prepared mustard

 Brown the bacon in a large saucepan. Cook and stir until completely browned. Remove and crumble. Set aside. Pour the pork and beans into the saucepan and add the wieners, catsup, tomato sauce, onion, honey and mustard. Blend well. Add the bacon and mix again. Cook on medium-low heat for 30-45 minutes, stirring occasionally. Serves 6.

Oven Barbecued Lamb Shanks

8 lamb shanks	1/2 t. salt
1/2 c. flour	1/2 t. black pepper
1 t. salt	1 c. catsup
1/4 c. vegetable oil	2 T. apple cider vinegar
1/2 c. brown sugar	15 oz. can crushed tomatoes
1 T. spicy Dijon mustard	hot, cooked rice

 Dredge the lamb shanks in the flour and salt. Heat the oil in a large ovenproof skillet or baking pan. Brown the lamb over medium-high heat, turning to brown evenly on all sides. Drain off any excess fat. In a small bowl, combine the brown sugar, mustard, salt, pepper, catsup and vinegar. Blend and pour over the lamb shanks. Add the tomatoes, cover and bake at 350°F for 2 hours, or until the lamb is very tender. Serve the lamb and sauce over the rice. Serves 8.

Maple & Apple Glazed Pork Chops

4 rib pork chops, 1-inch thick

1 T. vegetable oil

1 large green apple, peeled and cut into 4 thick slices

1/2 c. maple syrup

1/4 c. prepared barbecue sauce

2 T. lemon juice

2 T. Worcestershire sauce

1 T. cornstarch

1/4 c. water

salt and pepper to taste

Brown the pork chops in a large skillet in the oil over medium-high heat for 2-3 minutes. Season with salt and pepper to taste. Drain off the oil and any fat. Place 1 slice of apple on each chop. Combine the syrup, barbecue sauce, lemon juice and Worcestershire sauce in a small bowl and pour over the pork chops. Simmer, covered, for 45 minutes, or until the chops are cooked through and tender. Remove the chops to a serving platter. Mix together the cornstarch and water and stir into the sauce in the pan. Cook over medium-high heat, stirring constantly, until the sauce comes to a boil and is thickened. Remove from the heat and pass the warm sauce with the chops at the table. Serves 4.

Pork Chow Mein

2 lbs. lean pork, thinly sliced
1/4 c. cornstarch, divided
1 t. sugar
1/3 c. soy sauce
2 T. sesame oil
2 c. water
2 c. celery, sliced
1 large onion, sliced

1 clove garlic, minced
2 carrots, peeled and cut julienne-style
8 oz. can water chestnuts, sliced
4 oz. jar mushrooms, drained
2 c. fresh bean sprouts, cleaned and cut in half
4 green onions, thinly sliced
crispy Chinese noodles

 Mix the pork strips in a medium bowl with 2 tablespoons of the cornstarch, the sugar and 1 tablespoon of the soy sauce. Marinate for 30 minutes. Heat a large skillet or wok and add the oil. Fry the pork strips in the oil for 2 minutes. Add the remaining soy sauce and 1½ cups of water. Simmer for 10 minutes. Add the celery, onion, garlic and carrots, stirring to blend. Simmer for 5 minutes. Blend the remaining cornstarch with ½ cup of water and add to the meat and vegetables. Cook and stir over medium heat until the sauce is thickened and smooth. Add the water chestnuts, mushrooms, bean sprouts and green onions and toss well with the

other ingredients. Cook for 2-3 minutes, or until the vegetables are tender-crisp and heated through. Serve over crispy Chinese noodles and pass additional soy sauce, if desired. Serves 6.

Spicy Stuffed Lamb Chops

6 rib lamb chops, 2-inches thick
(double chops)

1 onion, chopped

2 cloves garlic, minced

1 c. Italian seasoned bread
crumbs

1/2 c. celery, finely chopped

pinch ground sage

1/4 t. black pepper

1/4 t. salt

1/4 c. butter or margarine, melted

1/2 lb. spicy Italian sausage,
cooked and crumbled

2 T. extra-virgin olive oil

1/2 c. chicken broth

1/2 c. canned crushed tomatoes,
Italian-style

 Cut a wide pocket in the side of each lamb chop, cutting as close to the bone as possible. In a large bowl, combine the onion, garlic, bread crumbs, celery, sage, pepper, salt, butter and sausage. Mix well to combine. The stuffing mixture should be somewhat compact and well-blended. Pack the stuffing firmly into each chop, allowing a bit to extend past the edges of the chop.

Heat the oil over medium-high heat in a large skillet or saucepan and add the chops. Brown the chops for 2 minutes. Turn and brown the chops for 2 minutes. Reduce the heat to medium-low, add the chicken broth and tomatoes and simmer for 30-40 minutes, or until the lamb is cooked to your preference. Serves 6.

Apple Cider Bratwurst & Sauerkraut

6 bratwurst sausages
3/4 c. apple cider
2 c. canned sauerkraut

2 t. caraway seeds
2 T. fresh parsley, minced

 Place the sausages in a large skillet and brown over medium-high heat for 5 minutes, turning to brown evenly. Add the apple cider and reduce the heat to medium-low. Simmer for 10 minutes. Add the sauerkraut and caraway seeds and cook, uncovered, for 5 minutes. Add the parsley and cook and stir for 2 minutes. Serve immediately. Serves 4.

Smoked Ham & Mushroom Risotto

1 T. butter or margarine

1 medium onion, finely chopped

1 clove garlic, finely minced

1 2/3 c. Arborio short-grain rice

2 15 oz. cans chicken broth

1/2 lb. mushrooms, cleaned and chopped

1 c. smoked ham, chopped

2 T. fresh parsley

 Melt the butter in a large saucepan or skillet and add the onion and garlic. Cook over medium-high heat for 2 minutes. Add the rice and cook, stirring constantly, until the rice is lightly browned. Add the chicken broth and reduce the heat to low. Simmer for 10 minutes. Add the mushrooms, ham and parsley and mix well with the rice mixture. Cover and simmer for 8-10 minutes, or until most of the broth is absorbed and the rice is tender. Serves 4.

Scalloped Ham & Cheese Potatoes

2 T. vegetable oil
1 small onion, chopped
6 medium potatoes, peeled and
   thinly sliced
1/4 t. salt

1/2 t. freshly ground black pepper
1 1/2 c. fully cooked ham,
   chopped
1/2 c. process cheddar cheese
   spread
1/4 c. half and half cream

 Heat the oil over medium-high heat in a large sauté pan and add the onion. Cook for 2 minutes. Add the potatoes, salt and pepper and cook on medium heat for 5-6 minutes, or until golden brown. Turn and cook for 1 minute. Add the ham and mix well. Combine the cheese spread with the cream in a blender and process until smooth. Pour the sauce over the ham and potatoes. Cook on very low heat, covered, for 5-6 minutes, or until heated through.

Prosciutto & Walnut Pesto Pasta

1 c. fresh basil
1/4 c. walnuts, chopped
1/4 c. extra-virgin olive oil
2 cloves garlic, minced
1/2 c. Parmesan cheese, grated
1/4 t. salt

water as needed
1 c. prosciutto, chopped
3 T. roasted red peppers, chopped
1 T. extra-virgin olive oil
8 oz. hot bowtie pasta, cooked
al dente

 Process the basil, walnuts, olive oil, garlic, cheese and salt in a blender until almost smooth. Add water, if needed, to make a good consistency. In a large serving bowl, combine the prosciutto, red peppers, oil and hot pasta, tossing well to combine. Add ½ cup of the pesto and toss again. Save the remaining pesto for another use. Garnish with additional Parmesan cheese, if desired, and serve immediately. Serves 4-6.

Pork Chili Verde

1 T. vegetable oil

1 lb. boneless pork loin, cut into small pieces

2 4 oz. cans green chilies, chopped

4 roma tomatoes, cored, seeded and chopped

1/4 c. purple onion, chopped

1/4 c. fresh cilantro, chopped

2 T. fresh lime juice

1/4 t. liquid hot sauce

15 oz. can black beans, undrained

sour cream for garnish

Using a large stockpot or saucepan, heat the oil and add the pork loin pieces. Sauté over medium-high heat for 2 minutes. Turn the meat and brown for 2 minutes on the other side. Reduce the heat to low and add the green chilies, tomatoes, onion, cilantro, lime juice, hot sauce and black beans. Mix well to combine. Cover and simmer over low heat for 2½ to 3 hours, stirring occasionally. To serve, spoon into individual bowls and garnish with dollops of sour cream. Serves 4.

Apple & Herb Roasted Pork

2 lbs. boneless rolled pork loin roast

1/2 t. salt

1/4 t. pepper

3 russet potatoes, peeled and sliced

1 yellow onion, peeled and sliced

3 carrots, peeled and cut into matchstick pieces

1/2 t. dried rosemary

1/2 t. dried thyme

2 T. fresh parsley, minced

4 c. apple cider

 Place the roast in a large baking pan. Rub with the salt and pepper. Place the potatoes, onion and carrots around the roast. Sprinkle the rosemary, thyme and parsley over the meat and vegetables and pour the apple cider over all. Cover tightly with aluminum foil and bake for 2 to 2½ hours, or until the roast is tender and the vegetables are well-roasted. Serves 6.

Greek Lamb in Pita Pockets

1 small yellow onion, chopped
1 clove garlic, minced
8 oz. can tomato sauce
1/2 t. salt
1/4 t. black pepper
1 small purple onion, thinly sliced
1 green onion, thinly sliced

1 lb. ground lamb
1 t. dried oregano
1/2 t. ground cumin
1/4 t. ground cinnamon
1/4 t. cayenne pepper
1/4 c. butter or margarine
4 pita pocket breads, cut in half

 Combine the yellow onion, garlic, tomato sauce and ¼ teaspoon salt in a small saucepan. Heat and stir over medium heat until the sauce boils. Reduce the heat and simmer for 10 minutes. In a medium skillet, combine the purple onion, green onion, lamb, oregano, cumin, cinnamon, cayenne pepper and ¼ teaspoon salt. Mix well and cook over medium heat for 3-4 minutes, or until the lamb is cooked through and the vegetables are tender-crisp. Spread butter inside each pita pocket and fill with equal portions of the lamb meat mixture. Add 1-2 tablespoons of tomato sauce to each pita pocket and serve immediately. Serves 4.

Pork Chops Marrakech

4 center cut pork chops, 1/2-inch thick

2 T. extra virgin olive oil, divided

1 clove garlic, minced

1/4 c. white onion, chopped

1/2 c. carrots, finely chopped

1/2 c. celery, finely chopped

5 1/2 oz. pkg. roasted garlic and mushroom couscous

1 1/2 c. chicken broth

2 green onions, thinly sliced

Heat the 1 tablespoon of the oil in a saucepan or skillet and add the pork chops. Brown the chops over medium-high heat for 2 minutes. Turn and brown the other side for 2 minutes. Remove from the pan. Add 1 tablespoon of oil to the pan, reduce the heat to medium and add the garlic, onion, carrots and celery. Cook for 3-4 minutes, stirring to coat the vegetables with the oil. Add the couscous and the seasoning packet, the chicken broth and green onions and bring to a boil. Reduce the heat to simmer, add the pork chops, cover and cook for 7-9 minutes, or until the chops are cooked through and the couscous is tender. Serves 4.

CHAPTER FIVE

One-Dish Dinners
Beginning with Fish
& Shellfish

White fish and shellfish have very delicate and mild flavors that are easily overwhelmed by other ingredients. In this chapter, mild fish is partnered with particularly subdued ingredients so that the most important flavors of the fish and shellfish remain. For example, *Elegant Shrimp & Crab Bake* calls for a cream of mushroom soup base and a sprinkle of onions. *Fresh Lobster & Shrimp Risotto* includes a white wine sauce and Arborio rice. *Sautéed Scallops & Mushrooms with Pine Nuts* relies on the earthy hints of mushrooms and shallots mixed with lemon juice to support the delicate sea scallops.

Rich-tasting fish with more oil and density, such as salmon and tuna, can take on the more vigorous herbs and spices and partner with such additions as tomatoes, spinach, broccoli and ripe olives. Try *Stuffed Salmon Pie with Creamy Dill Sauce, Seashore Fish Medley* and *Tuna & Sun-Dried Tomato Cream.* Experiment with these one-dish dinners and create new favorites for your family. Fish and shellfish are not only "good-for-you," they make "good-tasting" one-dish dinners any night of the week!

Elegant Shrimp & Crab Bake

2 green onions, thinly sliced

1/2 c. white onion, minced

2 T. butter or margarine

1/2 lb. cooked shrimp, cut in small pieces (or 7 oz. can shrimp, drained and chopped)

1 c. fresh crab, cooked and cut into small pieces (you may substitute frozen, thawed crab, if desired)

10 3/4 oz. can condensed cream of mushroom soup

1/3 c. milk

1/2 t. freshly ground black pepper

6 c. hot, cooked rice

1/2 c. Parmesan cheese, grated

 Sauté the green onions and white onion in the butter for 3-4 minutes, or until the onions are translucent. Set aside. In a large mixing bowl, combine the shrimp, crab, soup, milk and pepper and blend well. Lightly coat a 2 quart baking pan with cooking spray and pour the rice into the bottom of the dish. Spread the shrimp and crab sauce over the rice and top with the Parmesan cheese. Bake, covered, at 350°F for 20 minutes, or until the shrimp and crab are heated through and the sauce is absorbed. Serves 4.

Tuna Nicoise Bake

2 10 oz. pkgs. frozen chopped spinach, thawed and squeezed dry

2 T. onion, chopped

12 1/2 oz. can solid pack tuna, drained and flaked

6 hard-cooked eggs, sliced in 1/4-inch slices

2 10-3/4 oz. cans condensed cream of mushroom soup

1 c. dairy sour cream

1/4 c. butter or margarine, melted

2 c. sourdough bread crumbs (day-old bread)

salt and pepper to taste

Lightly coat a 9" x 13" baking dish with cooking spray. Spread the spinach evenly across the bottom of the pan. Sprinkle the onion over the spinach and scatter the tuna evenly over the onion. Layer the eggs over the tuna. Mix together the soup and sour cream and pour over the eggs. Toss the butter with the bread crumbs and sprinkle over the top of the dish. Bake at 350°F for 30-35 minutes, or until hot throughout. Serves 6.

Hot Crab Baguettes

1 lb. fresh cooked crabmeat, picked clean and cartilage removed (you may substitute frozen, thawed and drained crab, if desired)	1 T. white onion, chopped
	8 slices Swiss cheese
1/4 c. mayonnaise	1 long French baguette, cut into 4 pieces and sliced almost in half horizontally
3/4 c. dairy sour cream	(each piece should be about 5-6 inches in length)
2 T. pickle relish	

Preheat the oven to 350°F. Combine in a medium mixing bowl, the crabmeat, mayonnaise, sour cream, pickle relish and onion and mix well. Place 2 slices of Swiss cheese in each piece of bread and spoon equal portions of the crab mixture into each of the baguettes. Wrap each sandwich tightly in foil and bake for 7-10 minutes, or until the sandwiches are heated through and the cheese has melted. Serves 4.

Fresh Lobster & Shrimp Risotto

2 T. extra-virgin olive oil

1 c. celery, finely chopped

1 c. white onion, finely chopped

3 cloves garlic, minced

1/2 c. dry white wine

5 c. chicken broth

1 1/2 c. Arborio rice

1 t. Worcestershire sauce

1 t. salt

1/2 t. black pepper

1/2 lb. fresh lobster, cleaned and cut into small pieces

1/2 lb. fresh medium shrimp, cleaned and cut into small pieces

1/4 c. flat-leaf parsley, chopped

Heat the oil in a large saucepan and add the celery, onion and garlic. Cook over medium-high heat for 2-3 minutes, stirring occasionally. Add the wine and bring to a boil. Reduce the heat and add 1 cup of the broth and the rice, Worcestershire sauce, salt and pepper. Simmer until the broth has been absorbed. Add 1 cup of broth. Simmer until the broth has been absorbed. Continue adding the broth and simmering the rice. When the last cup of broth is added, include the lobster, shrimp and parsley. Simmer for 10 minutes, or until the rice has almost completely absorbed the broth and the seafood is cooked through. Serves 6.

Schezwan Shrimp Stir Fry

1 clove garlic, minced
2 T. Oriental chili sauce
2 T. dark soy sauce
1 carrot, peeled and thinly sliced
1/2 c. water chestnuts, sliced
1 c. canned miniature
   corn-on-the-cob

1/2 c. sugar snap peas, cleaned
   and ends trimmed
1 lb. large shrimp, cleaned,
   deveined and tails removed
6 c. hot, cooked rice
2 green onions, thinly sliced

 Using a large wok or skillet, heat the garlic with the chili sauce and soy sauce. Add the carrot, water chestnuts, corn-on-the-cob and sugar snap peas and stir-fry for 2-3 minutes, turning occasionally. Add the shrimp and cook, covered, for 3 minutes. To serve, mound the rice on a serving platter, pour the shrimp and vegetables with the sauce over the rice and garnish with the green onions. Serves 4.

Family-Style Shrimp Fried Rice

2 cloves garlic, minced

1 T. vegetable oil

3 T. soy sauce

1/2 t. freshly ground black pepper

1 carrot, peeled and finely chopped

1/2 lb. fresh uncooked shrimp, cleaned and cut into small pieces

4 c. hot, cooked rice

2 eggs, scrambled and chopped

4 slices bacon, cooked and crumbled

 In a large skillet, heat the garlic in the oil on medium-high heat and cook for 1 minute. Reduce the heat to medium and add the soy sauce and pepper. Add the carrot and shrimp and stir-fry for 3 minutes. Add the rice and toss to fully incorporate the other ingredients. Add the eggs and bacon and toss again. Serve immediately. Serves 4.

Creamy Crab Primavera

2 T. butter or margarine

2 T. flour

3 c. milk

1 t. salt

1/2 t. black pepper

2 c. instant rice

1 lb. cooked crabmeat, picked through and cartilage removed, shredded

1/2 c. broccoli florets, cooked to tender-crisp

1/2 c. baby carrots, cooked to tender-crisp

1/2 c. baby pearl onions, cooked to tender-crisp

1/2 c. red bell peppers, cooked to tender-crisp

1/2 c. mild cheddar cheese, grated

Make a roux in a large saucepan by combining the butter and the flour over medium heat. Stir constantly until the butter is melted and the mixture is thickened and smooth. Slowly add the milk, salt and pepper and bring to a boil, whisking to blend well. Boil for 1 minute. Remove 1 cup of the sauce and add the rice and crabmeat to the remaining 2 cups of sauce. Cover and let stand for 5 minutes. Add the broccoli, carrots, onions, peppers and remaining cup of sauce and stir well to blend all of the flavors. Cook for 2-3 minutes over medium heat or until all of the vegetables are heated through. Sprinkle with the cheddar cheese and let stand for 2 minutes. Serves 4.

Sautéed Scallops & Mushrooms with Pine Nuts

1 1/2 lbs. sea scallops, cleaned
1/4 t. salt
1/4 t. pepper
2 T. butter
2 T. extra virgin olive oil
3 c. button mushrooms, sliced
1/4 c. pine nuts, toasted

1/4 c. shallots, minced
1 clove garlic, minced
3/4 c. dry white wine
1/4 c. fresh lemon juice
1/4 c. fresh parsley, chopped
8 oz. angel hair pasta, cooked al dente
parsley for garnish

Pat the scallops dry with a paper towel. Sprinkle salt and pepper over each. Heat the butter and the oil in a large skillet over medium-high heat. Add the scallops, mushrooms and pine nuts. Stir-fry for 2 minutes, or until the scallops are cooked through. Remove the scallops from the skillet. Set aside and keep warm.

Place the shallots and garlic in the skillet and stir-fry for 30 seconds. Stir in the wine and the lemon juice. Bring to a boil and cook 3 minutes. Return the scallops to the skillet and cook for another 30 seconds. Serve over the angel hair pasta and garnish with the parsley, if desired. Serves 4.

Tuna & Sun-Dried Tomato Cream

1 1/2 lbs. fresh tuna fillets, cut into 4 pieces

2 T. sesame oil

4 green onions, thinly sliced

6 T. sun-dried tomato halves, reconstituted and chopped

1 c. half and half cream

1 lb. bowtie pasta, cooked al dente

1 t. salt

1/2 t. freshly ground black pepper

2 T. fresh parsley, minced

In a large skillet, heat the sesame oil and add the tuna fillets. Sear over medium heat for 2 minutes. Turn and sear again for 2 minutes. Cover and add ¼ cup of water and poach lightly for 5-6 minutes, or until the tuna is cooked medium-rare. Set aside and keep the fillets warm. In the same pan, add the green onions and sundried tomatoes and cook on medium heat for 3 minutes, allowing any remaining liquid to become absorbed. Add the cream, pasta, salt, pepper and parsley and toss lightly. To serve, mound the pasta on individual plates and top with the tuna fillets. Serves 4.

Maine Fisherman's Supper

1 1/2 lbs. Dover sole fillets

1 c. zucchini, thinly sliced

1 small purple onion, peeled and sliced into thin rings

1 red bell pepper, sliced into thin rings

12 oz. can Italian-style stewed tomatoes

1 t. salt

1/2 t. freshly ground black pepper

2 T. fresh parsley, minced

 Place the fillets in a 9" x 13" baking pan that has been lightly coated with cooking spray. Layer the zucchini, onion, bell pepper, stewed tomatoes, salt and pepper over the fish. Bake, covered, at 350°F for 25 minutes. Sprinkle the parsley on top and bake for 10 minutes. Serves 4.

Seashore Fish Medley

2 lbs. firm white fish fillets (halibut, red snapper, etc.), cut into 6 pieces

6 new red potatoes, peeled and cut into 1-inch chunks

1 c. celery, sliced into 1-inch pieces

2 carrots, peeled and sliced into 1-inch pieces

2 ripe tomatoes, cut into 1-inch pieces

1 T. fresh dill, chopped

3/4 c. mayonnaise

2 T. onion, finely minced

1 t. black pepper

1/2 t. salt

 Cut 6 foil squares, 10-inches on each side. Place 1 fish fillet on each foil square and top with equal portions of the potatoes, celery, carrots and tomatoes. Mix together in a small bowl, the dill, mayonnaise, onion, black pepper and salt and blend. Top each fish and vegetable foil square with 1 generous tablespoon of the dill sauce. Fold each foil square and seal completely. Bake at 375°F for 30-40 minutes, or until the fish flakes easily and the vegetables are cooked through. Serves 6.

Cheesy Baked Fish & Chips

1/2 c. butter or margarine, melted	1/4 t. salt
3 large baking potatoes, sliced	1/2 t. garlic powder
1/2 t. black pepper	2 T. fresh parsley, chopped
1/2 t. garlic powder	1 1/2 lb. firm, white fish fillets, cut
2 c. finely crushed cheese crackers	into 4 pieces
1/2 t. black pepper	

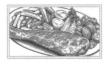 Pour half of the butter into a large 9" x 13" baking pan. Spread by tilting the pan to coat. Add the potatoes, sprinkle with the pepper and garlic powder and cover tightly with foil. Bake at 350°F for 20 minutes. Pour the remaining butter into a shallow plate. In another plate, combine the cracker crumbs, pepper, salt, garlic powder and parsley. Dip the fish fillets in the butter and then in the crumb mixture. Repeat to cover all sides of the fish. Remove the foil from the potatoes and push the potatoes to one side of the pan. Place the fish fillets in the pan and sprinkle the remaining crumb mixture over the potatoes and the fish fillets. Bake for an additional 15-20 minutes, or until the fish flakes easily. Serves 4.

Sea Bass en Brochette

12 oz. firm sea bass fillets, cut into 1-inch cubes

3 fresh zucchini, cut into 1-inch chunks

1 white onion, cut into 1-inch pieces

1 red bell pepper, cut into 1-inch pieces

20 large mushrooms, cleaned

2 cloves garlic, minced

2 T. fresh dill, chopped

1/2 c. balsamic vinegar

2 T. extra virgin olive oil

Preheat the broiler. Place the sea bass, zucchini, onion, red pepper and mushrooms on skewers, alternating each ingredient. In a small bowl, combine the garlic, dill, balsamic vinegar and olive oil. Place the skewers on the broiler pan and brush evenly with the marinade. Turn and brush again. Broil for 5-7 minutes. Turn, brush with the marinade and broil again for 4-6 minutes, or until the fish is cooked through and the vegetables are tender. Serves 4-6.

Stuffed Salmon Pie with Creamy Dill Sauce

2 c. crushed dry seasoned stuffing mix

1/2 c. butter or margarine, melted

1 c. chicken broth

2 eggs, beaten

1 t. spicy Dijon mustard

2 T. fresh parsley, chopped

1/4 c. onion, chopped

16 oz. can salmon, drained, picked through and cartilage and bones removed

Crumbly Crust:

1 c. crushed dry seasoned stuffing mix

1/2 c. butter, melted

Creamy Dill Sauce:

1/2 c.. dairy sour cream

1/4 c. prepared ranch dressing

1 T. fresh dill, chopped

2 T. milk

Mix together in a large bowl, the stuffing mix, butter, chicken broth, eggs, mustard, parsley, onion and salmon. Mix well. Pour into a 9-inch pie pan. Prepare the crust by combining the stuffing mix with the butter and sprinkling the mixture over the pie. Bake at 350°F for 40-45 minutes, or until heated through. To prepare the *Creamy Dill Sauce*, combine the sour cream, ranch dressing, dill and milk. Blend with a whisk. To serve, pour a small amount of the sauce over each piece of the salmon pie. Serves 6.

Seaside Cioppino

6 baby red potatoes, cut into large chunks

6 ears corn on the cob, cut into 2-inch pieces

2 large onions, cut into quarters

3 lbs. fresh crab claws

2 lbs. baby clams

1/2 c. fresh basil, chopped

1/2 c. fresh parsley, chopped

2 bay leaves

2 cloves garlic, minced

4 c. chicken broth

1 t. coarsely ground black pepper

1 t. kosher salt

1 loaf sourdough bread

Place the potatoes, corn, onions, crab and clams in a very large stockpot. Add the basil, parsley, bay leaves, garlic, chicken broth, pepper and salt. Heat to boiling, stirring occasionally. Reduce the heat and simmer for 40-45 minutes, or until the vegetables are heated through and the clams open. Discard any clams that do not open. To serve, ladle the fish, vegetables and broth into large bowls and serve with the sourdough bread. Serves 4-6.

Salmon & Olive Roll-Ups

1/4 c. celery, chopped

1/2 c. green bell pepper, chopped

1/2 c. onion, chopped

2 T. butter or margarine, cut into small pieces

1/2 c. ripe olives, chopped

16 oz. can red salmon, drained, picked through and bones and cartilage removed, flaked

10 3/4 oz. can condensed cream of chicken soup

1/2 t. salt

1/2 t. freshly ground black pepper

2 c. prepared baking mix

2/3 c. milk

1 T. sugar

1 egg, beaten

2 T. water

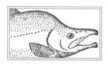 In a large bowl, combine the celery, green pepper, onion, butter, olives and salmon. Mix well to combine. Add ¼ cup of the soup, the salt and pepper. Mix with the salmon and vegetables.

Combine the baking mix with the milk and sugar to make a dough. Turn onto a lightly floured surface and roll to a rectangle 9" x 12" in size. Spread the salmon filling to within ½ inch of the edges and roll up as for a jelly roll, tucking in the ends securely. Place on a baking sheet, seam side down and bake at 400°F for 10 minutes. Combine the egg and water in a small bowl and brush over the dough. Bake for an additional 15-20 minutes. Remove the roll from the oven and cut into 1-inch slices. Serve immediately. Serves 4-6.

Homestyle Tuna Noodle Bake

12 1/2 oz. can tuna, drained

10 3/4 oz. condensed cream of mushroom soup

1/4 c. milk

1 t. black pepper

1/4 c. onions, chopped

12 oz. pkg. egg noodles, cooked al dente

2 c. crushed potato chips

 In a large mixing bowl, combine the tuna, soup, milk, pepper and onions. Add the noodles and mix well. Lightly coat an 8" x 8" baking pan with cooking spray and pour the tuna/noodle mixture into the pan. Top with the crushed potato chips and bake at 350°F for 30-35 minutes. Serves 4-6.

New Orleans Shrimp Creole

2 T. butter or margarine
1 green bell pepper, chopped
2 yellow onions, chopped
1/2 c. celery, chopped
1 lb. 4 oz. can whole tomatoes
1 t. salt
1/2 t. freshly ground black pepper
1/4 t. cayenne pepper

1 c. water
1 T. flour
1 t. sugar
2 c. fresh shrimp, cleaned, tails removed and cooked
1 c. frozen peas, thawed
8 c. hot, cooked rice

 Melt the butter in a large sauté pan and add the green pepper, onions and celery. Cook for 2-3 minutes, or until translucent. Add the tomatoes, breaking them up with a spoon slightly. Add the salt, pepper, cayenne pepper and water and bring to a boil. Reduce the heat and simmer for 10 minutes. Combine the flour and sugar and add 2 tablespoons of water, blending to make a smooth paste. Add to the herbs and vegetables, blending and stirring until thickened. Add the shrimp and peas and cook for 4-5 minutes. Serve hot over the rice. Serves 4-6.

Lobster & Brandy Linguine

4 cloves garlic, minced

2 T. extra virgin olive oil

2 T. brandy

15 oz. can diced tomatoes, undrained

1 t. dried basil

1/2 t. ground oregano

1/2 t. salt

1/2 t. freshly ground black pepper

1 lb. fresh lobster, cut into small pieces (you may substitute frozen, thawed lobster)

1 lb. linguine, cooked al dente

Asiago cheese for garnish

In a large saucepan, combine the garlic and olive oil and heat over medium-high heat for 2 minutes. Stir and add the brandy. Reduce the heat to medium and add the tomatoes, basil, oregano, salt and pepper. Stir and cook for 4-6 minutes. Add the lobster and cook for 5 minutes, or until the lobster meat is cooked through. Add the linguine and toss to mix well. Serve immediately and top with the Asiago cheese. Serves 4.

New England Clam Chowder

6 slices bacon

2 c. new red potatoes, cut into small cubes

1 c. carrots, peeled and cut into small cubes

1 c. onions, chopped

8 oz. can clams, undrained

2 T. flour

2 T. butter, melted

3 c. milk

1 c. half and half cream

2 t. freshly ground black pepper

1 t. salt

 Cook the bacon in a large stockpot until brown and crisp. Remove, crumble and set aside. Add the potatoes, carrots and onions to the stockpot, along with 2 cups of water. Heat to a gentle boil and cook for 15 minutes, or until the vegetable are soft. Add the clams and continue cooking. In a small bowl, make a paste of the flour and butter. Slowly blend the flour and butter paste into the hot soup until the soup is thickened and smooth. Add the milk and blend again. Add the cream and cook over medium-low heat for 3 minutes. Season with the salt and pepper and serve. Serves 6.

Crab-Stuffed Filet of Sole

4 large filets of sole
1 t. salt
1/2 t. pepper
1/2 c. fresh crab meat, bones and cartilage removed
1/2 c. fresh bread crumbs
3 green onions, chopped

1 T. fresh parsley, chopped
1 t. dried tarragon
2 T. fresh lemon juice
2 T. butter
2 T. flour
1 c. milk
1/2 c. dry white wine

 Salt and pepper each piece of fish. Combine in a small bowl, the crab, bread crumbs, onions, parsley, tarragon and lemon juice. Toss well. Spread equal portions of the crab stuffing on each piece of fish. Roll each piece of fish in jellyroll fashion and secure the ends with a toothpick. Place the fish rolls in a baking pan that has been buttered. In a medium saucepan, combine the butter and flour and stir constantly over medium heat until thickened. Slowly add the milk and white wine, stirring constantly, and continue cooking until thickened and smooth. Pour the sauce over the fish rolls, cover and bake at 350°F for 25 minutes. Serves 4.

CHAPTER SIX

Meatless One-Dish Dinners

Meatless dinners don't need to translate into "flavorless." Some of the best one-dish dinners start with beans, lentils or other protein sources. There are several choices in this chapter that will appeal to family members and guests alike, who may not even realize that meat is missing from the meal.

For hungry families, try *Country Shepherd's Pie, Italian Cheese Pie, Tomato Pesto Rigatoni* or *Hearty Lentil Soup*. When friends gather for dinner, consider *Italian Roasted Vegetables with Soft Polenta, Feta & Swiss Chard Frittata* and *Orzo-Stuffed Red Peppers*. Each of these dishes is designed to offer the best vegetables, whole grains, herbs and spices to complement your healthy lifestyle. Enjoy them all!

Italian Cheese Pie

1 lb. medium tofu sliced and drained

1 c. liquid egg substitute

1 c. lowfat cottage cheese

1/4 c. Parmesan cheese, grated, divided

1/4 c. onion, chopped

2 cloves garlic, minced

1 T. flour

3 T. fresh parsley, minced

1 t. ground oregano

1/2 t. black pepper

1/4 c. dry Italian-seasoned bread crumbs

1/4 c. butter or margarine, melted

Herb & Tomato Sauce

8 oz. can tomato sauce

2 T. canned tomato paste

2 roma tomatoes, chopped

1/2 t. ground oregano

1/4 t. dried basil

1/4 t. garlic powder

1/2 t. black pepper

Combine in a blender the tofu, egg substitute, cottage cheese, Parmesan cheese, onion, garlic, flour, parsley, oregano, black pepper and bread crumbs. Blend until very smooth. Coat a 10-inch pie pan with cooking spray and spread the mixture evenly on the bottom. Combine the bread crumbs with the melted butter and sprinkle over the top of the pie. Bake at 350°F for 30-35 minutes, or until set and lightly browned. To prepare the *Herb & Tomato Sauce*, combine the tomato sauce, paste, tomatoes, oregano, basil, garlic powder and pepper and cook over medium-low heat for 10 minutes. Simmer and stir to marry the flavors. To serve, slice wedges of the pie and spoon the sauce over each piece. Serves 4-6.

Meatless Fajitas

2 lbs. firm tofu, cut into thin strips

1 medium purple onion, thinly sliced

1 green bell pepper, thinly sliced

1 red bell pepper, thinly sliced

2 cloves garlic, minced

1 t. ground cumin

1 t. cayenne pepper

1 t. salt

1/2 t. chili powder

1 T. vegetable oil

12 6-inch flour tortillas

1 c. Jack cheese, shredded

1/2 c. dairy sour cream

2 green onions, chopped

Place the tofu, onion, peppers, garlic, cumin, cayenne pepper, salt and chili powder in a large, sealable plastic bag. Mix and refrigerate for 1 hour. To prepare the fajitas, heat 1 tablespoon of oil in a large sauté pan. Add the ingredients from the plastic bag and cook over medium heat for 4-6 minutes, stirring occasionally. Soften the tortillas in the microwave oven by wrapping in paper towels and heating on high for 1 minute. Fill each tortilla with 1 heaping tablespoon of the fajita mixture and garnish with the Jack cheese, sour cream and green onions. Serves 6.

Pan de la Hote

1 c. prepared baking mix	1/2 c. dairy sour cream
1 egg, beaten	1 lb. Jack cheese, sliced
1 T. sugar	7 oz. can whole green chilies
17 oz. can creamed corn	

 Combine the baking mix, egg, sugar, creamed corn and sour cream. Mix well until completely blended. Lightly coat a 1 quart baking pan with cooking spray and spread one-half of the creamed corn mixture evenly in the pan. Cover with one-half of the cheese slices. Top with one-half of the green chilies. Repeat the layers of creamed corn, cheese and green chilies. Bake for 20-35 minutes at 350°F, or until lightly browned and cooked through. Serves 6.

Old-Fashioned Farmer's Fry

4 russet potatoes, cooked and cubed

2 T. onion, chopped

2 T. vegetable oil

4 eggs

1/2 c. cheddar cheese, grated

salt and pepper to taste

 In a large ovenproof skillet, fry the potatoes over medium-high heat with the onion in the oil until the potatoes are crispy, about 5 minutes. Salt and pepper to taste. Crack each egg over the skillet, one in each quarter of the pan. Cover and cook until the eggs are set and cooked according to your preference. Sprinkle the cheddar cheese over the eggs and place under the broiler for 3-5 minutes, or until the cheese is bubbly. Serves 4.

Cheddar Tortilla Bake

12 6-inch corn tortillas, torn into small pieces
2 c. cheddar cheese, grated
2 T. flour
2 T. butter or margarine
3 T. chili powder

3 c. water
1 t. salt
1/2 c. prepared salsa
1 c. white onion, chopped
avocados for garnish

 Coat a 9" x 13" baking pan with cooking spray. Place one layer of tortillas on the bottom of the pan. Sprinkle with ½ cup of cheese and place another layer of tortillas over the cheese. In a medium saucepan, heat the flour and butter, stirring constantly, until thickened. Add the chili powder and slowly add the water and salt, stirring well to blend again. Remove from the heat. Spread about half of the salsa over the tortillas and pour one-half of the sauce over the salsa. Place another layer of tortillas over the sauce, pour the remaining salsa over the tortillas and top with the remaining sauce and cheese. Bake, uncovered, at 350°F for 25-30 minutes, or until heated through and bubbly. Serves 6.

Pearl Barley & Winter Vegetable Stew

2 T. butter or margarine
2 T. extra virgin olive oil
1 medium onion, diced
5 c. vegetable stock
1/2 lb. whole baby carrots
1/2 lb. baby parsnips
1/3 c. pearl barley
1 bay leaf
2 zucchini, cut into 1/4-inch slices
1 small cauliflower, cut into florets
1/4 lb. snow peas
1 T. dried Italian seasoning

1 t. fresh thyme, chopped
1/4 c. fresh parsley, chopped

Herb Dumplings:
1 c. flour
2 t. baking powder
1/2 t. salt
1/4 t. black pepper
1 T. dried Italian seasoning
1/2 c. milk
2 T. extra virgin olive oil

Make the dumplings by sifting the flour, baking powder, salt and pepper together in a mixing bowl. Add the Italian seasoning. Combine the milk and oil and add all at once to the dry ingredients, stirring just until moistened. Cover and set aside.

Melt the butter and oil in a large flameproof baking dish. When the butter begins to foam, add the onions and cook for 3-5 minutes until soft. Add the stock, carrots, parsnips, barley and bay leaf and bring to a boil. Cover and bake in a 375°F oven for 30 minutes. Remove the pan from the oven and stir in the zucchini, cauliflower, snow peas, Italian seasoning, thyme and parsley. Season with salt and pepper to taste. Drop heaping tablespoons of the dumpling batter on the stew. Cover the pan and return to the oven for 15-20 minutes, or until the dumplings are baked through. Remove the bay leaf and serve immediately. Serves 4.

Italian Roasted Vegetables with Soft Polenta

2 c. water	1/4 t. black pepper
2/3 c. yellow cornmeal	2 T. extra virgin olive oil
1 c. mozzarella cheese, shredded	2 red bell peppers
1/4 c. Parmesan cheese, grated	1 green bell pepper
2/3 c. heavy cream	1 portabella mushroom, sliced into thin pieces
1 t. salt	1 medium onion, sliced

 In a medium saucepan, bring the water to a boil. Add the cornmeal slowly, stirring constantly. Cook over medium heat for 2-3 minutes. Reduce the heat and add the mozzarella cheese, Parmesan cheese, cream, salt and pepper and blend very well. Lightly coat a 10-inch pie pan with cooking spray and spread the polenta over the bottom and sides of the dish. Mix together the olive oil, red peppers, green pepper, mushroom and onion and pour over the polenta, spreading the vegetables evenly. Cover and bake at 325°F for 25-30 minutes, or until the vegetables are soft and cooked through. Serves 4.

Feta & Swiss Chard Frittata

4 baking potatoes, baked
2 T. extra virgin olive oil
1 T. butter or margarine
1/2 c. purple onion, finely chopped
1 c. mushrooms, sliced
4 cloves garlic, minced
1 bunch Swiss chard, washed and chopped

8 eggs
8 oz. feta cheese, crumbled
1/4 c. fresh basil, chopped
1 t. fresh thyme, chopped
1/2 t. fresh oregano, chopped
1/2 t. salt
1/4 t. pepper
2 T. Parmesan cheese, grated

Slice the potatoes in ¼-inch rounds and set aside. Preheat the oven to 350°F and coat a 10-inch round baking dish with cooking spray. Heat the oil and the butter in a medium saucepan and sauté the onion and mushrooms until soft. Add the chard and garlic and sauté until the chard is bright green, about 4 minutes. In a bowl, combine the eggs, feta cheese, basil, thyme, oregano, salt and pepper. Arrange the potato slices in the bottom of the prepared dish. Spoon the chard mixture over the potatoes. Pour the egg and cheese mixture over the chard and top with the Parmesan cheese. Bake about 30 minutes, or until a knife inserted in the center comes out nearly clean. Serves 6.

Country Shepherd's Pie

4 baking potatoes, peeled and cut into chunks	1/2 c. celery, chopped
1 t. salt	1 c. parsnips, peeled and cut into chunks
1/2 t. black pepper	1 c. Brussels sprouts, cleaned and cut in half
1 c. warm milk	1 c. turnips, cut into chunks
1/4 c. butter or margarine	1/2 c. fennel, chopped
1 c. cheddar cheese, grated	1/2 t. fresh rosemary, minced
2 T. extra virgin olive oil	1/2 t. fresh thyme, minced
1 white onion, chopped	3 c. vegetable broth
1 clove garlic, minced	

 Cook the potatoes in a large pot of water over medium heat until soft, about 15 minutes. Drain the water from the potatoes, return the potatoes to the pot and add the salt, pepper, milk and butter. Mash with a hand masher or electric mixer until smooth. Add the cheese and mix again, adding more milk if necessary. Set aside.

Preheat the oven to 350°F. In a heatproof baking dish, place the oil, onion and garlic and mix gently. Put the dish in the oven for 5-7 minutes, or until the vegetables are soft. Remove and add the celery, parsnips, Brussels sprouts, turnips and fennel. Gently combine with a large spoon. Add the rosemary, thyme and vegetable broth and stir again. Cover and cook for 10-15 minutes, or until the vegetables are soft. Uncover and spread the mashed potatoes over the top of the dish, creating an even top layer. Return to the oven for 5-10 minutes, or until the potatoes a lightly browned. Serves 6.

Orzo-Stuffed Red Peppers

4 red bell peppers, cut in half, seeds and core removed

1/4 c. extra virgin olive oil

1 clove garlic, minced

1 small white onion, chopped

1 small tomato, chopped

1 1/2 c. cooked orzo

1 t. salt

1/2 t. black pepper

1/2 t. ground oregano

1/4 t. ground thyme

1 T. fresh parsley, minced

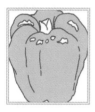 Preheat the oven to 400°F. Coat a large baking pan with cooking spray and arrange the pepper halves in the pan. Sauté the garlic and onion in the olive oil until soft, about 3 minutes. Add the tomato, orzo, salt, pepper, oregano, thyme and parsley and mix well. Lightly pack each bell pepper half with the orzo and herbs. Bake, covered, for 25-30 minutes, or until the peppers are soft. Serves 4.

Pasta e Fagioli

16 oz. can crushed tomatoes, Italian-style

19 oz. can cannelloni beans, rinsed and drained

1/2 c. fresh green beans, trimmed and cut into 1-inch lengths

1 small white onion, chopped

2 cloves garlic, minced

5 c. vegetable broth

1 small zucchini, cut into thin slices

1 c. uncooked small shell macaroni

1 t. salt

1 t. black pepper

1/2 t. crushed red pepper

Parmesan cheese for garnish

Combine in a large stockpot the tomatoes, beans, green beans, onion, garlic and vegetable broth. Stir over medium heat for 6 minutes. Add the zucchini, macaroni, salt, black pepper and red pepper and stir again. Simmer for 20 minutes to combine the flavors. Sprinkle Parmesan cheese over each serving. Serves 4.

Santa Fe Tamale Pie

1/2 c. vegetable oil	2 c. yellow cornmeal
1 c. yellow onion, chopped	1 t. baking powder
1 c. canned whole kernel corn	
1 c. canned diced tomatoes	**Chili Pepper Sauce:**
1 c. ripe olives, sliced	8 oz. can tomato sauce
3 cloves garlic, minced	8 oz. water
1/2 t. salt	1 T. green pepper, chopped
3 T. ground chili powder	1 T. cornstarch
3 eggs, beaten	2 t. ground chili powder
1 1/4 c. milk	1/2 t. salt

 In a large sauté pan, heat the oil and add the onion, corn, tomatoes, olives and garlic. Sauté for 4-6 minutes. In a medium bowl, blend the salt, chili powder, eggs, milk, cornmeal and baking powder until smooth. Coat an 8" x 10" baking pan with cooking spray and pour the vegetables into it. Pour the egg/cornmeal mixture over the vegetables and gently stir. Bake at 350°F for 30 minutes.

Prepare the *Chili Pepper Sauce* by combining in a small saucepan the tomato sauce, water, green pepper, cornstarch, ground chili powder and salt. Heat and stir until boiling. Reduce the heat and simmer for 5 minutes. To serve, pour the sauce over the individual portions of tamale pie. Serves 4-6.

Brunch Eggs Newport

6 eggs, hard-cooked

10 3/4 oz. condensed cream of mushroom soup

1/2 c. milk

1/2 c. mayonnaise

1 c. cheddar cheese, grated

6 English muffins, split and toasted

12 spears fresh asparagus, steamed to tender-crisp

 Lightly coat a 9" x 9" baking pan with cooking spray. Layer the eggs on the bottom of the pan. Mix together the soup, milk, mayonnaise and cheddar cheese and pour over the eggs. Bake at 350°F for 20 minutes. To serve, spoon the eggs and sauce over the English muffins. Top each muffin half with a spear of asparagus. Serves 6.

Sesame Sweet & Sour Brown Rice

1/4 c. rice wine vinegar
3 T. sesame oil
1 T. sugar
pinch cayenne pepper
6 c. brown rice, cooked

1/4 c. green onions, thinly sliced
1 c. celery, sliced
1/2 c. vegetable broth
2 T. almonds, chopped

 Preheat the oven to 350°F. In a large bowl, combine the vinegar, oil, sugar and cayenne pepper. Add the brown rice, onions, celery, vegetable broth and almonds. Mix well and turn into an 8" x 8" baking pan. Bake uncovered for 20-25 minutes, or until heated through. Serves 4.

Broccoli & Potatoes Au Gratin

1 c. canned white beans, rinsed and drained	1 T. onion, chopped
1/3 c. milk	1/2 t. prepared Dijon mustard
1/4 c. canned pimento, chopped	1 t. salt
3 T. nutritional yeast flakes	1/2 t. black pepper
3 T. tahini	1/2 lb. fresh broccoli, cut into small florets
1 T. lemon juice	1/2 lb. baking potatoes, cut into small cubes

Combine the beans, milk, pimento, yeast flakes, tahini, lemon juice, onion, mustard, salt and pepper in a blender and process until smooth. Arrange the broccoli and potatoes evenly in a large baking pan and pour the sauce over the vegetables. Cover and bake at 350°F for 35-40 minutes, or until hot throughout. Makes 4 servings.

Wild Rice Pilaf with Warm Peanut Sauce

4 c. cooked wild rice
1/2 c. onions, chopped
1/2 c. mushrooms, sliced
1/4 c. celery, chopped
1/2 c. smooth peanut butter

1 T. sweet white miso
1 t. fresh ginger, grated
pinch cayenne pepper
1/2 c. hot water

Lightly coat a 9" x 9" baking pan with cooking spray. Spread the rice on the bottom of the pan and add the onions, mushrooms and celery. Process the peanut butter, miso, ginger, cayenne pepper and hot water in a blender until very smooth. Add more water, if necessary. Pour the peanut sauce over the rice and vegetables and bake, covered, at 350°F for 30 minutes. Serves 4.

Tomato Pesto Rigatoni

1/2 c. sun-dried tomatoes, reconstituted and chopped

4 cloves garlic, minced

1/3 c. fresh basil, chopped

1/2 t. dried rosemary

1/4 c. Parmesan cheese, grated

1 c. vegetable broth

16 oz. rigatoni, cooked al dente

Parmesan cheese, grated

Salt and pepper to taste

 Place the tomatoes, garlic, basil, rosemary and cheese in a blender and process until smooth. Add salt and pepper to taste. In a large sauté pan, heat the vegetable broth. Add the pesto and stir to combine. Add the cooked rigatoni and toss well, adding Parmesan cheese to garnish. Continue cooking over medium heat for 3-5 minutes or until the ingredients are heated through. Serves 4.

Wild Mushroom & Onion Polenta

1 lb. prepared polenta roll	1/2 c. green onions, sliced
4 T. extra virgin olive oil, divided	1/2 c. water
6 oz. shiitake mushrooms, sliced	2 T. cornstarch
1 c. vegetable broth	1 t. salt
2 T. dry sherry	1/2 t. freshly ground black pepper

 Slice the polenta in rounds ½-inch thick. Heat 2 tablespoons of the oil in a large sauté pan and add the polenta. Fry the slices for 2 minutes or until lightly browned, and turn and fry to brown the other side. Remove the polenta from the pan and keep warm.

Sauté the mushrooms in 2 tablespoons of the oil in the sauté pan for 3-4 minutes, turning once. Add the broth, sherry and green onions and cook over medium heat for 4-5 minutes to reduce the sauce. Mix the water and the cornstarch in a cup and slowly add to the broth mixture. Add the salt and pepper. Heat and stir for 2 minutes, or until the sauce is thickened and smooth.

To serve, arrange the polenta slices on individual plates and pour the mushroom sauce over each serving. Serves 4.

Rice & Black Bean Soup

2 c. long grain white rice, cooked
1 c. canned tomato juice
3 c. vegetable broth
15 oz. can black beans, drained

16 oz. can crushed tomatoes, Italian-style
1 t. black pepper
mozzarella cheese for garnish

In a large stockpot, combine the rice, tomato juice, broth, beans, tomatoes and black pepper. Heat and stir until boiling. Reduce the heat and simmer for 15 minutes. Top individual bowls with mozzarella cheese to garnish. Serves 4.

Fresh Vegetable Lasagna

4 T. extra virgin olive oil, divided

4 cloves garlic, minced

1 onion, minced

16 oz. can diced tomatoes

16 oz. can tomato sauce

1/4 c. dry red wine

1/2 t. dried oregano

1/2 t. dried basil

1/2 t. dried marjoram

1/2 t. dried thyme

1 t. salt

1/2 t. freshly ground black pepper

1 red bell pepper

1 medium zucchini, thinly sliced

10 oz. crimini mushrooms, cleaned and sliced

6 oz. fresh spinach, washed and chopped

16 oz. part-skin ricotta cheese

1/4 c. milk

1 lb. lasagna noodles, cooked and drained

8 oz. pkg. mozzarella cheese, grated

 Heat 2 tablespoons of oil in a large saucepan and add the garlic and onion. Sauté for 2 minutes. Add the diced tomatoes, tomato sauce, red wine, oregano, basil, marjoram, thyme, salt and pepper. Mix well and simmer for 10 minutes, stirring occasionally. Remove from the heat and pour the sauce into a large bowl.

In the same saucepan, heat 2 tablespoons of oil and add the bell pepper. Heat for 2 minutes. Add the zucchini and mushrooms, cooking and stirring over medium heat. Add the spinach and cook just until the spinach is wilted. Remove from the heat. Heat the oven to 350°F. In a small bowl, combine the ricotta cheese and milk. To assemble the lasagna, spread a bit of sauce on the bottom of a 9" x 13" baking pan. Place one layer of noodles over the sauce. Top with ⅓ of the vegetables and cover with ⅓ of the cheese. Repeat the layers of sauce, noodles, vegetables and cheese. Top all with the mozzarella cheese. Cover and bake for 35-45 minutes, or until the lasagna is hot throughout. Serves 8.

Pad Thai Noodles

3 T. peanut oil, divided
3 eggs, beaten
1 lb. rice or udon noodles, cooked al dente
4 cloves garlic, minced
1 lb. fresh bean sprouts
6 green onions, thinly sliced
1/2 t. dried red pepper flakes
1/2 c. fresh cilantro, chopped
1/2 c. peanuts, chopped

Coconut Sauce:
1 c. coconut milk
1/3 c. catsup
3 T. brown sugar
juice of 1 lime
1/4 c. soy sauce

Prepare the *Coconut Sauce* by combining the ingredients in a small bowl. Whisk together and set aside. Heat 2 tablespoons of the oil in a large sauté pan and add the eggs. Cook and stir until set. Flip and cook until set on the other side. Remove from the heat and cut the eggs into thin strips. Heat 1 tablespoon of the oil in the pan and add the garlic, sprouts and green onions. Add the red pepper flakes and mix well. Steam and stir for 5 minutes. Add the cooked noodles, eggs and coconut sauce and heat and stir again for 3 minutes. Stir in the cilantro and peanuts and serve immediately. Serves 4-6.

Hearty Lentil Soup

1 T. extra virgin olive oil
2 yellow onions, chopped
1 green bell pepper, chopped
2 cloves garlic, minced
2 carrots, peeled and thinly sliced
2 celery stalks, sliced
1 c. dried lentils, sorted and rinsed
2 bay leaves
1 t. ground paprika
1/2 t. dried oregano

1/2 t. dried basil
1/2 t. dried thyme
6 c. water
28 oz. can pureed tomatoes
1/4 c. dry red wine
1 c. small shell pasta, uncooked
1 1/2 t. salt
1 t. freshly ground black pepper
Parmesan cheese for garnish

Heat the olive oil in a large stockpot and add the onions and pepper. Heat and stir for 2 minutes. Add the garlic, carrots and celery and stir and heat for 2 minutes. Add the lentils, bay leaves, herbs and water. Stir. Heat to boiling over medium high heat. Reduce the heat and add the tomatoes and red wine. Simmer for 40 minutes. Add the pasta, salt and pepper and heat for 15 minutes. To serve, ladle the soup into bowls and top with the Parmesan cheese. Serves 4.

Vegetable Lo Mein with Crispy Noodles

2 T. sesame oil

8 oz. pkg. prepared coleslaw vegetables

1 c. fresh crimini mushrooms, sliced

1 c. fresh green beans, trimmed and cut into 1-inch slices

1 c. fresh bean sprouts

3 green onions, thinly sliced

1/2 c. vegetable broth

1/2 t. freshly ground black pepper

8 oz. Chinese wheat noodles, cooked al dente

4 oz. Chinese crispy noodles, warmed

 Heat the sesame oil in a large sauté pan and add the coleslaw vegetables. Heat and stir for 3 minutes. Add the mushrooms, green beans, bean sprouts and onions and mix well. Stir-fry until the vegetables are tender-crisp, about 5 minutes, adding broth as needed to keep the vegetables from sticking to the pan. Sprinkle with the pepper and toss. Add the Chinese wheat noodles and toss. Serve immediately and garnish with the crispy noodles. Serves 4.

Pasta Aglia Olio

1/4 c. extra virgin olive oil

10 cloves garlic, minced

1 lb. fettucini pasta, cooked al dente

1/2 c. Parmesan cheese, grated

1/4 c. fresh parsley, chopped

1/2 t. salt

1/2 t. freshly ground black pepper

 Heat one-half of the olive oil in a large skillet and add the garlic. Cook over medium heat until softened. In a large pasta serving bowl, combine the cooked pasta with the remaining oil, along with the garlic and oil from the skillet. Add the Parmesan cheese, parsley, salt and pepper. Toss well and serve immediately. Serves 4.

CHAPTER SEVEN

Summertime One-Dish Dinners

The recipes in this chapter provide everything you need to enjoy a complete dinner, however they are served cold or at room temperature. Herbs and spices are especially flavorful when allowed to marry with pasta, potatoes or rice and the addition of a bit of meat or poultry can provide all you need for a quick and enjoyable cold repast.

For any day of the week, consider *Italian Vegetable Salad* or *Super Bean Salad*. Add a peasant bread and fruit for dessert and the meal is complete! When the days are especially warm and you want to escape the heat of the kitchen, try the *Hoisin Oriental Chicken Plate*, *California Flank Steak Salad* or *Ginger Chicken & Grape Salad*.

When you find leftover meat, poultry or seafood, try adding a pasta that you have on hand, toss in some fresh summer vegetables for color and texture and toss the salad with a prepared bottled dressing for a super-fast and inviting one-dish dinner. It all adds up to delicious meals in minutes!

Surfer Chicken Salad

2 c. chicken breast, cooked and torn into strips

2 c. frozen peas, thawed and drained

1 medium tomato, cut into thin wedges

1 small green pepper, cut into thin slices

1 small red pepper, cut into thin slices

1 small purple onion, peeled and cut into very thin rings

1 c. mayonnaise (prepared or homemade)

1 t. sugar

2 T. almonds, roasted and sliced

salt and pepper to taste

 In a large serving bowl, layer the chicken breast pieces, peas, tomato, peppers, and onion. Sprinkle with a bit of salt and pepper. Smooth the mayonnaise completely over the top of the salad. Sprinkle the sugar lightly over the mayonnaise. Refrigerate 8 hours or overnight. To serve, toss well and garnish with the almond slices. Serves 4.

Ginger Chicken & Grape Salad

1 c. mayonnaise	2 c. seedless red grapes
1 t. rice wine vinegar	1 c. celery, sliced
1/2 t. ground ginger	1/2 c. water chestnuts, sliced
1/2 t. salt	1/4 c. green onions, thinly sliced
1/2 t. freshly ground black pepper	1/2 c. walnuts, coarsely chopped
3 c. chicken, cooked and sliced into thin strips	romaine lettuce leaves

 In a mixing bowl, combine the mayonnaise, vinegar, ginger, salt and pepper. Mix thoroughly. Add the chicken, grapes, celery, water chestnuts, onions and walnuts. Mix well again. Line a large serving bowl with the romaine lettuce leaves and place the salad in the bowl. Cover tightly and refrigerate for 1 hour. Serves 4.

Hoisin Oriental Chicken Plate

2 chicken breasts, cooked and chopped

1/2 head green cabbage, finely shredded

2 green onions, thinly sliced

1/4 c. almonds, slivered

1 pkg. instant ramen noodles

Hoisin Dressing:

2 T. hoisin sauce

1/2 c. sesame oil

3 T. rice wine vinegar

2 T. sugar

1 t. salt

1/2 t. freshly ground black pepper

 In a large serving bowl, combine the chicken, cabbage, onions and almonds. Crush the ramen noodles and add to the chicken and vegetables. Toss until well-mixed. In a small bowl, combine the hoisin sauce, sesame oil, vinegar, sugar, salt and pepper. Pour the *Hoisin Dressing* over the salad and toss again. Chill the salad in the refrigerator for at least 1 hour before serving. Serves 6.

Italian Vegetable Salad

10 oz. pkg. frozen Italian-style cut green beans, cooked and drained	1/4 c. green onions, sliced
	1/4 t. ground oregano
3 c. elbow macaroni, cooked al dente	1/2 t. black pepper
	1/2 t. salt
1 c. carrots, shredded	1/2 c. Italian garlic and cheese salad dressing
1 c. celery, sliced	Asiago cheese for garnish

 In a large serving bowl, combine the beans, macaroni, carrots, celery and onions. Toss with the oregano, pepper and salt. Drizzle the salad with the Italian dressing, tasting as you pour to adjust the dressing to the salad. Serve at room temperature or refrigerate for 1 hour. Garnish with the Asiago cheese to serve. Serves 4.

Turkey Pasta Salad
with Roasted Red Pepper Dressing

2 c. turkey, cooked and shredded into small pieces

1 small zucchini, cut into thin slices

1 small purple onion, peeled and cut into thin rings

10 cherry tomatoes, halved

1 green pepper, sliced

1 lb. farfelle pasta, cooked and drained (or your choice of salad pasta)

6 oz. jar fire-roasted peppers

3 T. lemon juice

3/4 c. dairy sour cream

1/2 t. kosher salt

1/2 t. freshly ground black pepper

 Combine the turkey, zucchini, onion, tomatoes, green pepper and pasta in a large serving bowl. Using a blender, mix the peppers, lemon juice, sour cream, salt and pepper until smooth and well-blended. Pour the dressing over the turkey salad and toss well to combine. Refrigerate for 1 hour before serving. Serves 4.

Greek Lamb & Potato Salad

1 c. cooked lean lamb, cut into 1/2-inch cubes	1/2 c. dairy sour cream
2 c. new red potatoes, cooked and cut into small cubes	2 T. lemon juice
	1 T. extra virgin olive oil
1 c. fresh green beans, cooked and cut into 1-inch pieces	1 t. sugar
	1 t. Dijon mustard
1/2 c. black olives, sliced	1 clove garlic, minced
2 eggs, hard-cooked and sliced	salt and pepper to taste

Combine the lamb, potatoes, green beans, olives and eggs in a large serving bowl. Whisk together the sour cream, lemon juice, olive oil, sugar, mustard and garlic and blend completely. Add salt and pepper to taste. Pour the dressing over the lamb and potato salad and chill prior to serving. Serves 4.

California Flank Steak Salad

2 lbs. beef flank steak	2 green onions, thinly sliced
2 T. extra virgin olive oil	2 cloves garlic, finely minced
1 t. cracked black pepper	2 T. fresh parsley, finely minced
1/2 t. salt	1/8 t. crushed red pepper
8 oz. angel hair pasta, cooked and drained	1/2 c. extra virgin olive oil
	2 T. balsamic vinegar
3 small zucchini, thinly sliced	1 t. dried basil
1 orange or red pepper, thinly sliced	1/2 t. dry mustard
	1/4 t. salt

 Season the flank steak with the 2 tablespoons of olive oil and the salt and cracked black pepper. Grill or broil the steak until medium rare, about 6 minutes on each side. Slice across the grain very thinly and set aside. Combine together in a large mixing bowl, the pasta, zucchini, orange pepper, onions, garlic and parsley. Toss gently. In a shaker jar, combine the crushed red pepper, olive oil, vinegar, basil, mustard and salt and toss well. Lightly dress the salad. Add the beef slices and toss gently again. Serves 6.

Spicy Thai Chicken & Vegetable Vermicelli

Spicy Peanut Sauce:

1/2 c. smooth peanut butter

1/2 c. soy sauce

2 T. rice wine vinegar

1 T. sesame oil

1/4 t. hot chili oil (or more, if desired)

1 t. crushed red pepper flakes

1 t. ground ginger

1 T. water

1/2 lb. cooked chicken breast, shredded

1 c. broccoli florets, cooked to tender-crisp

1 red pepper, thinly sliced

1/2 c. green onions, sliced

1/4 c. fresh cilantro, chopped

1/3 c. dry-roasted peanuts, coarsely chopped

1 lb. vermicelli pasta, cooked and drained

Prepare the sauce by combining the ingredients in a blender and processing until very smooth. In a large serving bowl, combine the chicken, broccoli, red pepper, green onions, cilantro and peanuts. Mix well. Add the pasta and mix again. Pour the peanut sauce over the vermicelli and toss until the ingredients are evenly coated. Chill for 1 hour before serving. Serves 4-6.

Super Bean Salad

6 oz. canned green beans, sliced

8 3/4 oz. can kidney beans, rinsed and drained

8 3/4 oz. can garbanzo beans, rinsed and drained

1 1/2 c. canned black beans, rinsed and drained

1 red bell pepper, chopped

1 clove garlic, minced

1 small purple onion, cut into thin rings

1/4 c. extra virgin olive oil

1/4 c. apple cider vinegar

1 t. sugar

1 t. salt

1/2 t. freshly ground black pepper

2 T. fresh parsley, minced

 In a large serving bowl, toss together the green beans, kidney beans, garbanzo beans and black beans. Add the bell pepper, garlic and onion and mix again. In a small bowl, combine the olive oil, vinegar, sugar, salt and pepper and whisk vigorously. Pour the dressing over the salad and combine thoroughly. Cover and refrigerate for at least 1 hour. Note: you may add cooked, chopped chicken breast meat or cooked beef tenderloin slices to this salad for additional flavor and protein. Garnish with the parsley to serve. Serves 4.

Mediterranean Lamb Couscous

2 c. quick-cooking couscous

1 3/4 c. vegetable broth

2 T. extra virgin olive oil

2 green onions, thinly sliced

1/2 c. fresh snow peas, thinly sliced

1/2 c. carrots, diced fine

1/2 c. red bell pepper, finely chopped

1 lb. cooked lean lamb, thinly sliced

1 clove garlic, minced

2 T. balsamic vinegar

1/4 t. salt

1/4 t. black pepper

Place the couscous in a large serving bowl. Heat the broth to boiling and pour over the couscous. Add the olive oil, cover and let stand for 5 minutes. Uncover the couscous and fluff with a fork. Add the green onions, snow peas, carrots, bell pepper and lamb. Sprinkle with the garlic, vinegar, salt and pepper and toss all ingredients lightly. Serve at room temperature. Serves 4.

CHAPTER EIGHT

Extra Quick
& Extra Easy
One-Dish Dinners

What could be easier than combining a few simple ingredients along with fresh herbs or spices? In this chapter, you will find the recipes you need when time is at an absolute minimum and you have a hungry family waiting. To minimize some of the time required to make these dinners, you can also prepare many of these items prior to the time when you actually need them. For example, try chopping several onions at once and saving the onions you don't immediately need in a sealed plastic bag in the refrigerator. Roast more than one chicken or cut of beef at a time and refrigerate the leftovers for sumptuous meals during the busy weeknights. Keep your pantry well-stocked and have items on hand for quick recipe variations as needed.

Better than fast-food and more nutritious overall, a quick and tasty one-dish dinner is the best touch to even the busiest day!

Stockpot Chicken with Spring Vegetables

4 chicken breast halves, skinless
  and boneless

1 T. extra virgin olive oil

1 yellow onion, chopped

1 c. whole baby carrots

15 oz. can diced tomatoes,
  undrained

1 t. salt

1/2 t. black pepper

1/2 t. chili powder

15 oz. can whole new potatoes,
  cut in half

10 oz. pkg. frozen green beans

1 c. canned or frozen whole
  kernel corn

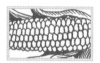 Chop the chicken into small chunks. In a large stockpot, brown the chicken in the olive oil over medium heat for 2 minutes. Turn and brown again. Reduce the heat and add the onion, carrots, tomatoes, salt, pepper and chili powder. Stir well and simmer for 8 minutes. Add the new potatoes, green beans and corn and stir again. Simmer for 5-8 minutes, or until the soup is heated through and the vegetables are tender-crisp. Serves 4.

Cantonese Garlic Chicken

1 lb. chicken breast, cut into thin strips

1 T. soy sauce

1 T. garlic, minced

2 T. sesame oil

16 oz. pkg. frozen mixed vegetables (Chinese or Japanese)

1/3 c. water

1 T. cornstarch

1/4 c. soy sauce

6 c. hot, cooked rice

freshly ground black pepper to taste

 Using a large sauté pan, fry the chicken, soy sauce and garlic in the sesame oil for 2 minutes. Add the frozen vegetables and cook for 3 minutes. In a medium measuring cup, combine the water and cornstarch and mix well. Add the soy sauce. Pour over the chicken and vegetables and stir until the sauce is slightly thickened and the vegetables and chicken are cooked through. Add pepper to taste. Serve over the hot rice. Serves 4.

Turkey & Walnut Couscous with Cranberry Sauce

6 oz. pkg. couscous pasta
1 1/4 c. water
1 T. butter or margarine
1 1/2 c. cooked turkey, cubed
1/4 c. walnuts, chopped

1/2 t. black pepper

Cranberry Sauce:
1 c. canned cranberry sauce
2 T. fresh apple juice

Combine the couscous, water and butter in a large saucepan. Bring to a boil. Add the seasoning packet from the couscous, the turkey, walnuts and pepper and stir to combine. Remove the saucepan from the heat and allow it to stand for 7 minutes. In a 2-cup glass measuring cup, heat the cranberry sauce and apple juice in the microwave oven for 1 minute on high. Spoon the sauce over the cooked turkey couscous. Serves 4.

Hurry-Up Turkey Tenderloin

10 3/4 oz. can condensed cream
of mushroom soup

1/4 c. half and half cream

10 oz. pkg. frozen spinach,
thawed and squeezed dry

6 large slices turkey tenderloin

1/2 c. Parmesan cheese, grated

freshly ground black pepper to
taste

 Lightly coat a 9" x 13" baking pan with cooking spray. Combine the cream of mushroom soup with the cream and pour half of the mixture into the bottom of the pan. Arrange the spinach evenly over the soup and cover the spinach with the turkey slices. Pour the remaining soup mixture over the turkey. Spread the cheese over all. Cover and bake at 350°F for 20-25 minutes, or until the turkey is cooked completely through. Serves 4-6.

Chicken Mexicana

3 c. cooked chicken, cubed
4 green onions, finely sliced
7 oz. green chilies, chopped
2 12 oz. cans cream of chicken
  soup

2 c. dairy sour cream
6 oz. seasoned tortilla chips
4 oz. cheddar cheese, shredded

 Lightly coat a 2 quart baking pan with cooking spray. In a large bowl, combine the chicken, onions, chilies and cream of chicken soup. Mix thoroughly. Add the sour cream and mix again. Place the tortilla chips in the bottom of the baking pan and pour the chicken over the chips. Sprinkle the cheddar cheese over the chicken. Bake, uncovered, at 350°F for 30 minutes. Serves 6.

Super-Easy Chicken Pot Pie

1 c. cooked chicken breast, cut into cubes
3 c. frozen mixed vegetables of your choice
12 oz. cream of mushroom soup
1 t. salt
1/2 t. black pepper
1/2 t. ground oregano
1 c. prepared baking mix
3/4 c. milk
1 egg
2 T. butter, melted
1/4 c. Jack cheese, shredded

Lightly coat a 9-inch pie pan with cooking spray. Layer the chicken, vegetables, soup, salt, pepper and oregano in the pan. In a medium bowl, mix together the baking mix, milk and egg. Pour the baking mixture over the chicken and vegetables. Drizzle the butter and Jack cheese over the baking mixture. Bake, uncovered, at 400°F for 30-40 minutes, or until golden brown and cooked through. Serves 4.

Paprika Chicken & Rice

10 3/4 oz. cream of mushroom
  soup

1 1/2 c. water

1 c. long grain white rice,
  uncooked

1/2 c. onions, chopped

1/4 t. paprika

1/2 t. salt

1/4 t. black pepper

4 chicken breast halves, skinless
  and boneless

 Lightly coat a baking pan with cooking spray. Mix together the soup, water, rice, onions, paprika, salt and pepper. Pour the sauce and rice into the baking pan. Add the chicken breast pieces over the mixture and cover tightly. Bake at 375°F, or until the chicken is cooked through completely. Serves 4.

Easy Spanish Rice

4 c. hot, cooked long grain white rice

16 oz. can tomato sauce

1/2 small white onion, chopped

1 green bell pepper, chopped

3 mild Italian sausages, cooked

1 t. ground chili powder

1/2 t. salt

 Combine the rice, tomato sauce, onion and green pepper in a mixing bowl and blend well. Cut the sausages into small pieces and add to the rice and vegetables. Sprinkle the rice with the chili powder and salt and mix again. Coat a large baking pan with cooking spray and spread the sausages and rice in the pan, smoothing the top evenly. Bake at 350°F for 15 minutes or hot throughout. Serves 4.

Jiffy Chili Beans 'N' Cornbread

1 c. canned chili beans
8 oz. can tomato sauce
1 yellow onion, chopped
2 T. ground chili powder
1/2 t. salt

1/2 lb. ground beef, cooked and crumbled
8 oz. pkg. cornbread mix
1 c. milk
1 egg, beaten

In a large baking pan, stir together the chili beans, tomato sauce, onion, chili powder, salt and ground beef. Preheat the oven to 350°F. In a small bowl, mix the cornbread mix, milk and egg and spread the batter evenly over the chili. Bake, uncovered, for 30 minutes, or until the cornbread is completely cooked and the chili is heated through. Serves 4.

Onion Baked Chicken & New Potatoes

6 new red potatoes, cut into
   chunks

8 pieces chicken, as desired

10 3/4 oz. can condensed cream
   of chicken soup

1/2 c. chicken broth

1 pkg. dry onion soup mix

Place the potatoes in the bottom of a 9" x 13" baking pan. Arrange the chicken pieces over the potatoes. In a small bowl, mix together the soup, broth and dry onion soup mix. Pour the soup mixture over the chicken and potatoes. Cover tightly with aluminum foil and bake at 375°F for 45-55 minutes, or until the chicken is cooked through completely and the potatoes are tender. Serves 4.

Chinese Tuna Bake

7 oz. can solid white tuna, drained

1 c. celery, chopped

2 green onions, chopped

10 3/4 oz. can condensed cream of mushroom soup

1/4 c. milk

2 c. crispy Chinese noodles

1 c. canned water chestnuts, sliced

2 T. soy sauce

Combine the tuna, celery, onions, soup and milk in a large mixing bowl. Preheat the oven to 350°F. Place the Chinese noodles in the bottom of a 9" x 9" baking pan. Mix the water chestnuts and soy sauce into the tuna mixture and pour over the noodles. Bake, uncovered, for 30 minutes. Serves 4.

Super Tostada Skillet

16 oz. can refried beans
1/4 t. ground cumin
1 c. cooked lean beef, cut into
 thin slices
1/4 c. prepared taco sauce
1 c. cheddar cheese, shredded

1/4 c. green onions, thinly sliced
1 tomato, chopped
1 T. fresh cilantro leaves
salsa for garnish
8 prepared corn tostada shells

 Spread the refried beans in the bottom of a large skillet. Sprinkle with the ground cumin. Heat the beans over medium heat until warmed and slightly steaming, stirring occasionally. Spread the beans into an even layer and top with the beef. Pour the taco sauce over the beef. Sprinkle the cheddar cheese over the sauce. Cover and cook on medium heat for 5-6 minutes, or until the cheese is melted and the tostada is cooked through. Layer the green onions over the cheese, spread the tomato evenly over the onions and top with the cilantro. To serve, divide the skillet into fourths and scoop equal portions of the tostada filling onto the tostada shells. Garnish with salsa. Serves 4.

Chuckwagon Sloppy Joes

1 lb. lean ground beef
1 c. onion, chopped
1 green bell pepper, chopped
8 oz. can tomato sauce

3 T. prepared barbecue sauce
4 onion rolls, split and toasted
4 slices American cheese

 Brown the ground beef in a skillet and drain any excess fat. Add the onion and green pepper and cook over medium heat for 4 minutes. Add the tomato sauce and barbecue sauce and mix well, stirring to blend. Cook and stir for 3-4 minutes, or until slightly thickened and hot. Spoon the meat and sauce equally over the rolls and top each sandwich with a slice of American cheese. Serve immediately. Serves 4.

Asiago Linguine

8 oz. fresh linguine noodles	2 cloves garlic, minced
2 T. extra virgin olive oil	1/2 c. Asiago cheese, grated
1 red bell pepper, finely chopped	2 T. fresh parsley, minced

 Cook the noodles in boiling water until just tender. Drain and place the noodles in a large serving bowl. Add the olive oil, red pepper, garlic, cheese and parsley. Toss well and serve immediately. Serves 3-4.

Rainy Day Cheese & Potato Soup

2 10-3/4 oz. cans condensed
  cheddar cheese soup

1 c. cream

1 c. milk

8 oz. can Mexican corn

8 oz. can potatoes, drained

2 green onions, sliced

1/2 t. salt

1/2 t. black pepper

 Combine the cans of soup, cream and milk in a large saucepan. Cook on medium heat, stirring to blend, for 3-4 minutes. Add the Mexican corn. Heat for 2 minutes. Roughly chop the potatoes and add to the soup. Add the salt and pepper and stir well. Simmer for 10 minutes. Serves 4.

Tortellini Florentine

28 oz. jar prepared spaghetti
   sauce
4 1/2 oz. jar mushrooms, sliced
1 lb. fresh cheese tortellini (you
   may substitute frozen, thawed
   tortellini)

10 oz. pkg. frozen chopped
   spinach, thawed and squeezed
   dry
1/2 c. Parmesan cheese, grated

Coat a 2 quart baking pan with cooking spray. Pour enough spaghetti sauce on the bottom of the pan to cover. Add one half of the mushrooms. Layer one half of the cheese tortellini over the mushrooms and spread one half of the spinach over the tortellini. Pour one half of the remaining sauce over the spinach. Repeat the layers of mushrooms, tortellini, spinach and sauce. Spread the Parmesan cheese over the sauce and bake, covered, at 350°F for 30-35 minutes, or until heated through and bubbly. Serves 4-6.

Divine Chicken Divan

4 chicken breast halves, skinned
  and boned

10 3/4 oz. can condensed cream
  of chicken soup

1/2 c. milk

1 t. salt

1/2 t. black pepper

16 oz. pkg. frozen broccoli spears,
  thawed and drained

6 c. hot, cooked brown rice

Parmesan cheese for garnish

 Coat the bottom of a medium baking pan with cooking spray. Place the chicken breast pieces in the pan. Mix together the soup and milk and add the salt and pepper. Pour one half of the soup/milk mixture over the chicken. Layer the broccoli spears over the soup and add the remaining soup over the broccoli. Sprinkle grated Parmesan cheese over the top of the dish. Bake, uncovered, at 350°F for 25-30 minutes or until the chicken is completely cooked through. Spoon the chicken and sauce over the hot rice to serve. Serves 4.

Pork Loin Chops with Wild Rice Pilaf

4 pork loin chops, 3/4-inch thick	1 white onion, finely chopped
2 T. extra virgin olive oil	1 large tomato, finely chopped
6 T. wild rice	1/2 c. green bell pepper, chopped
6 T. long grain white rice	2 1/2 c. beef broth
6 T. thin vermicelli noodles, broken into 1-inch pieces	1/4 t. dried marjoram
	1/4 t. dried thyme

Brown the chops in the olive oil in a large skillet. Turn and brown for 2 minutes. Remove from the heat and set aside. Coat a 2 quart baking dish with cooking spray and spread the wild rice, white rice and noodles in the bottom of the dish. Layer the onion, tomato and green pepper over the pilaf. Place the pork chops over the pilaf. Pour the beef broth over the pork and vegetables and sprinkle the herbs over all. Cover and bake at 350°F for 1 hour, or until the pork is fully cooked and the rice has absorbed most of the liquid. Serves 4.

Scalloped Pork Chops

3 large baking potatoes, peeled
10 3/4 oz. condensed cream of
   mushroom soup

1/2 c. milk
4 pork shoulder or loin chops
1/2 c. cheddar cheese, grated

 Coat a 2 quart baking pan with cooking spray. Use a cheese grater to finely shred the potatoes. Layer the potatoes in the bottom of the pan. Mix the soup with the milk and pour over the potatoes. Place the chops over the soup mixture. Bake, uncovered, at 350°F for 60-65 minutes. Serves 4.

Confetti Chicken & Rice

1/4 c. butter or margarine	1 c. cooked chicken, chopped
1 1/2 c. quick-cooking brown or white rice	1 c. green onion, chopped
2 10-1/2 oz. cans chicken broth or consommé	1 c. carrots, peeled and finely chopped
1/2 t. salt	1 c. celery, chopped
	1/4 c. almonds, sliced

 Melt the butter in a large flameproof baking pan and add the rice. Cook over low heat, stirring occasionally, for about 5 minutes. Add the broth and salt. Heat to boiling. Remove from the heat and place in the oven. Bake at 350°F for 20 minutes. Add the chicken, green onion, carrots, celery and almonds and stir lightly to combine. Bake for an additional 10 minutes. Serves 4.

Pepperoni Pizza Bagels

6 oz. can tomato paste
1 t. ground oregano
5 fresh bagels, split
1/2 c. onion, chopped

1/2 c. green bell pepper, chopped
1 c. pepperoni slices, chopped
1 c. mozzarella cheese, shredded

 Preheat the oven to 450°F. Combine the tomato paste and oregano in a small bowl. Spread equal portions of the tomato sauce over each of the bagel halves and arrange the bagel halves on a baking sheet. Top each bagel with onions, green peppers and the chopped pepperoni. Sprinkle the cheese over each bagel. Bake for 6-8 minutes and serve immediately. Serves 5.

Ham & Fusilli Supper

2 c. uncooked fusilli pasta	2 c. cooked ham, cubed
1/2 c. mushrooms, sliced	2 T. balsamic vinegar
1 red bell pepper, chopped	4 T. extra virgin olive oil
1/2 c. ripe olives, sliced	1 t. black pepper
1/2 c. cheddar cheese, cut into small cubes	1/2 t. salt

Cook the fusilli pasta in salted boiling water until al dente. Drain and immediately pour the pasta into a large serving bowl. Add the mushrooms, red pepper, olives, cheddar cheese and ham and toss lightly. In a small bowl, mix together the balsamic vinegar, olive oil, pepper and salt. Pour over the pasta and toss well. Serve immediately. Serves 4.

Hungarian Goulash

1 lb. lean ground beef
1 white onion, chopped
8 oz. can tomato sauce
1 t. chili powder

1/2 t. black pepper
15 oz. can whole kernel corn
8 oz. wide egg noodles, cooked
    and drained

 Brown the ground beef in a skillet, stirring occasionally, until no pink remains. Drain any excess fat. Add the onion and heat for 2 minutes, stirring twice. Add the tomato sauce, chili powder, pepper, corn and egg noodles and toss thoroughly. Heat for 5-10 minutes, stirring occasionally, until all ingredients are heated and cooked through. Serves 4.

Quick Shrimp Alfredo

1 lb. medium shrimp, cleaned and deveined, tails removed

2 T. extra virgin olive oil

12 oz. refrigerated alfredo sauce

1 t. freshly ground black pepper

2 T. fresh parsley, minced

8 oz. angel hair pasta, cooked and drained

1/4 c. Asiago cheese, grated

 In a large skillet, sauté the shrimp in the olive oil until pink and cooked through, about 4-6 minutes. Add the prepared alfredo sauce, pepper and parsley and stir and heat. Serve the shrimp alfredo over the angel hair pasta and sprinkle Asiago cheese over all. Serves 4.